T0305219

# Teaching Entrepreneurship to Postgraduates

David Sydney Jones

1938–2013

*O, my cherished father*

# Teaching Entrepreneurship to Postgraduates

Colin Jones

*University of Tasmania, Australia*

**Edward Elgar**
Cheltenham, UK • Northampton, MA, USA

Published by
Edward Elgar Publishing Limited
The Lypiatts
15 Lansdown Road
Cheltenham
Glos GL50 2JA
UK

Edward Elgar Publishing, Inc.
William Pratt House
9 Dewey Court
Northampton
Massachusetts 01060
USA

A catalogue record for this book
is available from the British Library

Library of Congress Control Number:   2013946804

This book is available electronically in the ElgarOnline.com Business Subject Collection, E-ISBN 978 1 78347 260 4

ISBN      978 1 78100 474 6

Printed and bound in Great Britain by T.J. International Ltd, Padstow

# Contents

# Figures

# Foreword

Entrepreneurship educators constantly face the challenge of finding new and innovative approaches to make the entrepreneurship phenomenon comprehensible and applicable to the lives of their students. Our students are not a homogeneous group and differ for example in education, age, nationality and professional experience.

After his successful first book *Teaching Entrepreneurship to Undergraduates*, Colin Jones now addresses such challenges with the lively and multifaceted sequel, *Teaching Entrepreneurship to Postgraduates*. His many years of experience as an entrepreneur and entrepreneurship educator allow him to investigate in a unique way which specific teaching and learning approaches are relevant and adequate for postgraduates in contrast to undergraduates. He argues that diversity and the postgraduates' various life experiences can be integrated into the learning context in a useful way. He emphasizes the importance of interactive teaching in cooperation with the students and of giving them space for personal learning experiences. Such an open learning environment may offer the chance of transforming entrepreneurial opportunities. Therefore *action* in the sense of an entrepreneurial action-orientation and *interaction* in entrepreneurial networks are at the core of the consideration. In the education of postgraduates, entrepreneurship educators are facilitators rather than teachers. However, since there is no *one size fits all* solution, this volume with its 12 chapters is meant to inspire readers to think about the particularities of entrepreneurship education for postgraduates. In doing so, they may discover starting points for the development and improvement of their own teaching and learning concepts.

Colin Jones has made an effort to integrate the comprehensive experiences of renowned international entrepreneurship educators found globally throughout the respective chapters. In addition, he deals with more recent entrepreneurship concepts such as the effectuation approach. Reading this book will be worthwhile and inspiring to all who wish to gain insights in the multiple facets and characteristics of state-of-the-art entrepreneurship education for postgraduates.

Prof. Dr. Christine Volkmann
Schumpeter School of Business and Economics, University of Wuppertal

# Introduction

It would be too bold to claim that my previous recent work *Teaching Entrepreneurship to Undergraduates* (Jones, 2011) is the intellectual ancestor of this current work. It would be more accurate to state that having walked some distance in one direction on the left hand side of the road, it is now time to return to my original staring point a little wiser; and walk some distance in the same direction, but on the right hand side of the road. I anticipate that this alternative journey will be just as fulfilling in terms of creating moments of reflective opportunity. I sense the greatest challenge we will face is in giving our students sufficient credit for the entrepreneurial behaviours they have already demonstrated in their busy lives. Perhaps, the ultimate challenge for us all is to recognise that we all have the capacity to be entrepreneurs, just perhaps not the types who typically become famous.

The Nobel Peace Prize winner and micro finance pioneer Muhammad Yunus has been widely credited with observing that we are all in fact entrepreneurs. Staring out originally as cave dwellers we were all self-employed, responsible for finding food and feeding ourselves. His assertion being that we gradually lost these innate abilities as civilisation emerged and we increasingly became someone else's labor. As Labor we have forgotten that we were once all entrepreneurs; capable of solving all manner of problems related to our survival.

Putting to one side the potential implications of defining entrepreneurship in such a primitive manner, the point is well made; we are all innately capable of entrepreneurial behaviour. However, I find it easy to draw parallels between the participation of adults in entrepreneurship and love in society. On one hand, the challenge of love, accepting our inability to predict it and/or encourage it so as to sustain it. All we can state is that at any time in society love will be present, but we can't say with accuracy much more than that. Equally, the presence of entrepreneurship in society, while ever-present, remains a mystery as well. However, this book aims to consider the opportunities and challenges that educators collide with whilst interacting with postgraduate students of entrepreneurship; those studying at any level higher than a bachelor degree.

Whilst the primary context of this book is situated in Higher Education, it is the intention of this work to view our adult students as learners embedded in specific and individual life journeys. My focus is not on the nature of the curriculum required to assist multiple cohorts learn to be more entrepreneurial. Rather, concern is given to allowing individual students make sense of their life, its constraints, opportunities and the process of reconnecting to their 'inner caveperson'.

In terms of starting this journey a little wiser, the process of writing *Teaching Entrepreneurship to Undergraduates* has made me both more appreciative and understanding of the various contexts of entrepreneurship education, hereinafter referred to as EE. From the conversations and invited interactions I have had with enterprise educators and students the world over; I gratefully acknowledge an intellectual debt. My past concerns for the legitimacy of our collective practice have been realised in my own backyard, further heightening my awareness of the fragility of our ability to practice our craft for the betterment of our students' development. The differences between this work and *Teaching Entrepreneurship to Undergraduates* arise from contextual differences directly related to the dissimilarities that exist between undergraduate and postgraduate students. It must be always remembered that in the absence of a single mode of selection (that is, regulatory best practice), there will be a natural tendency for increasing complexity of teaching and learning practice in EE. As I have stated elsewhere (Jones and Matlay, 2011), this is to be celebrated as it what makes EE so unique. However, it is critically important that we are all capable of explaining this diversity of practice, as it is germane to our contextual environment. That is the intended contribution of this work, to arm you with the ability to understand the various needs of your students and to be able to justify your approach to satisfying their needs.

The motivation for this work is to provide a distinct sister volume to *Teaching Entrepreneurship to Undergraduates*. The first volume sought to promote a learner-centred approach to thinking about how to teach entrepreneurship to undergraduates. This volume seeks to define the difference in thinking between teaching entrepreneurship to postgraduates as opposed to undergraduates. Therefore, a common structure is retained across both volumes, with attention given to both subtle and major differences between the motivation and process of learning related to entrepreneurship education for postgraduates and undergraduates. It is hoped that this sister volume will be as distinctive and innovative in terms of its constant focus on challenging issues, possible solutions to those challenges (based both the author's practice and that of other educators situated in various global contexts), and probing questions to prompt reflection of your own teaching practice. I will again be including the views of other entrepreneurship educators globally to gain a broad spectrum of opinions germane to the issues under discussion. Before we proceed, let us first consider the purpose of each chapter.

## CHAPTER SUMMARIES

### Chapter 1   Your Teaching Philosophy

The first chapter is focused on the educator's teaching philosophy. The key differences from the first volume will be the consideration given to how and why our teaching philosophies may differ between undergraduate and postgraduate situations. I aim to help you understand who you are relative to the process of EE and your students' aspirations. To assist this aim, I will also include the opinions of other educators within the first chapter and conclude with several reflective questions to provoke deeper thinking. I hope to ensure you adopt a reflective disposition during this chapter. A disposition that I hope you serves you well throughout the entire book.

### Chapter 2   Nascent Entrepreneurship and Adults

The second chapter is focused on the nascent entrepreneur and adults as learners. The aim of this chapter is to situate the process of entrepreneurship within the lives of our adult learners. How have they been entrepreneurial thus far and how might they be entrepreneurial in the future? How do adults differ from adolescent learners? What motivations do they exhibit as mature learners? So the emphasis is on moving from pedagogy to andragogy. I hope to convince you that the use of fixed curriculums in EE reduces our ability to respond to our students' varied aspirations. I will again include the opinions of other educators within the chapter and conclude with an array of reflective questions to provoke deeper thinking.

### Chapter 3   The Situational Dilemma

The third chapter deals with the situational factors that mature students uniquely share. The front cover of this book hints at an analogy of environmentally induced change. I hope to inspire you to see your students and your interaction with them in new and exciting ways. Your students have accumulated many life experiences and the diversity and experiences of each student you meet represent the raw ingredients of their profitable learning opportunities. The challenge therefore being to consider how we as educators can best use this diversity to their advantage in terms of developing and awakening entrepreneurial potential. To succeed, I argue that you must be capable of facilitating transformational learning experiences. Essentially, I argue you must be able to motivate and challenge your students in the right way to be effective. I will again include the opinions of other educators within the chapter and conclude with a range of reflective questions to provoke deeper thinking.

## Chapter 4 The Tethered Adventurer

The fourth chapter deals with what type of graduate are we might be trying to create? If the idea of the reasonable adventurer were not appropriate for postgraduates, what might be? I will explore the notion of the tethered adventurer, seeking to capture the reality of the lives from which many of postgraduate students are embedded in. My approach here is not to convince you of what type of graduate to create, rather I am urging you to step back and contemplate what type of graduate would be appropriate for your individual context. Again, issues related to the diversity within the class vis-à-vis their reasons for studying will be discussed. I will include the opinions of other educators within the chapter and conclude with several reflective questions to provoke deeper thinking.

## Chapter 5 Exploiting Student Experience

The fifth chapter considers the experience that each student has accumulated and how this may be used to benefit the cohort's learning outcomes. Reference is made to what I call the *Harvard factor* to illuminate this issue. Unlike undergraduate students, postgraduates come equipped with a different range of vocational experience, experience that can be leveraged and exchanged throughout the learning experience. I want to challenge you to relinquish your authority in your classroom. I want you to enrol your students into leadership and educator roles. I will again include the opinions of other educators within the chapter and conclude with an array of reflective questions to provoke deeper thinking.

## Chapter 6 The Extended Learning Environment

The sixth chapter considers the nature of the extended learning environment, students as learners who visit (or return to) the classroom, rather than students seeking to graduate from the classroom. There are many implications that arise from recognising the nature of the open boundaries that surround our students as mature learners. I want you to contemplate the challenging implications of employing experiential education approaches. I want you to consider the *places* where learning occurs. Further, to consider what our learners will actually be *doing* when they are learning. I will again include the opinions of other educators within the chapter and conclude with an array of reflective questions to provoke deeper thinking.

## Chapter 7   The Resource Profile

The seventh chapter continues the first volume's consideration of the students' resource profiles. Rather than merely considering the limitations of age, the challenges of auditing and creating awareness of whom and what is actually known is considered. Also, the nature of what capacity exists to access vital resources related to anticipated forms of entrepreneurial behaviour. I will again include the opinions of other educators within the chapter and conclude with an array of reflective questions to provoke deeper thinking.

## Chapter 8   Seeing the World Differently

The eighth chapter considers the issue of how our students make sense of the world they live in. The environmental interaction framework I have developed is introduced and discussed. I contend the greatest gift your students will ever give you will be a glimpse of their dreams. The responsibility that comes with this gift is enormous. Overstate their likelihood of success and we risk causing them future pain, understate the potential value of the idea and we risk introducing future anxiety. While we cannot know the future in advance, we can surely move our students closer to their future, hopefully providing them with a clearer view of what may lay ahead. I will again include the opinions of other educators within the chapter and conclude with yet more reflective questions to provoke deeper thinking.

## Chapter 9   Believing and Knowing

The ninth chapter seeks to bridge a gap between 'old style' 20th century opportunities and 21st century opportunities and the skills related to observing and exploiting such opportunities. The low-cost of web-enabled EE is discussed from the perspective of how we as educators can facilitate a shift in student confidence. Confidence related to how our students can embrace the raft of low-cost opportunities related to their potential entrepreneurial opportunities. Within this chapter I will present detailed accounts of how leading EE educators are exploiting technology to the advantage of their students.

## Chapter 10  Ideas and Business Plans

The tenth chapter considers the evaluation of our students' ideas, of assisting them to step out and embrace the reality of their markets, communities and end-users. The aim is to present a non-prescriptive framework for enabling our students to act and then plan rather than planning to act. The benefits of not completing a business plan will be weighed against the potential gains from completing a business plan. The key issue of (study) time is accounted for in this regard with consideration given to the priorities of their educational outcomes; student choice being a critical issue to be contemplated. I will again include the opinions of other educators within the chapter and conclude with many reflective questions to provoke deeper thinking.

## Chapter 11  Connecting for Action

The eleventh chapter deliberately sets out to be highly provocative through the initial introduction of Carlos Castaneda's *path with a heart*. Why haven't our postgraduate students entered the fray of entrepreneurial bedlam? What would compel them to do so post their interaction with their entrepreneurial educational experience? My experiences tell me that there are many paths our students could tread; yet there are only a few that they should (or could) travel. Returning to many of the issues canvassed in the first three chapters, factors of a personal nature to each student are reintroduced to propose a strong foundation for contemplating sustainable entrepreneurial behaviour. Throughout this chapter I will again share my students' feelings with you to provide a context of the adult learners I work with.

## Chapter 12  You are not Alone

The twelfth and final chapter contemplates current and future challenges we as entrepreneurship educators face when working with postgraduate students. Unlike the mist that shrouds our undergraduates from the immediate reality of their future, our postgraduate students arrive seemingly simultaneously ensconced in their past, present and foreseeable future. Many seek assistance and knowledge that may have a very short shelf life. Our ability to mentor their development is paramount and we need to be either very talented or very connected to satisfy their needs. This chapter aims to revisit my personal observations of the challenges we face (teaching postgraduates), as discussed throughout this book. It is important to appreciate that every educator's practice is not developed overnight, but rather through trial and error processes occurring over many years. You are entitled to be less than perfect in the development of your approach. I hope you enjoy the journey that awaits you. I offer my thoughts not as a suggestion of any form of best practice, but rather as a context against which you can reflect upon.

# PART I

# Scoping the Issues

# 1.   Your Teaching Philosophy

Among all men [or women], whether of the upper or lower orders, the differences are eternal and irreconcilable, between one individual and another, born under absolutely the same circumstances. One ... made of agate, another of oak; one of slate, another of clay. The education of the first is polishing; of the second, seasoning; of the third, rending; of the fourth, moulding. It is of no use to season the agate; it is vain to try and polish the slate. (Ruskin, 1917: 198)

The above quote resonates with my way of thinking about teaching adult postgraduate learners. When I step out of the undergraduate context and into the postgraduate context, it is as if I have been parachuted into a multiplex cinema blindfolded. I have no knowledge of what is playing, what genres are on offer, when the movies started and when they will finish. In contrast, by and large my undergraduate students have arrived before me with similar motives (i.e. to establish a career) and have travelled essentially quite similar educational journeys thus far (sadly, predominantly as passive learners). So while there is diversity in all my teaching contexts, I see increased levels of diversity in my postgraduate cohorts. Recognition of this fact will permeate through all chapters and guide my interaction with the other contributors to this work.

## REVISITING MY TEACHING PHILOSPHY

In *Teaching Entrepreneurship to Undergraduates* (Jones, 2011: 10) I discussed in detail the development of my teaching philosophy. To avoid repeating what has been previously stated, I remarked that 'I am trying to ensure they are constantly walking in the entrepreneur's shoes (Gibb), always in their here and now (Whitehead) whilst developing a sense of what they could be (Baxter-Magolda) through the development of key attributes related to their capacity to create opportunities for personal satisfaction (Heath) from an iterative reflective process (Tyler)'. At a meta-level, little has changed. However, the tools and processes used to enact my over-arching aims have substantially changed.

I still subscribe to the view that entrepreneurs are *found* in society, rather than merely *born* and/or subsequently *made*. The key difference I observe with postgraduate students is that they need assistance to identify with the role of entrepreneur. This I believe is at the heart of our role, allowing our students to reconceptualise their presence in society. Thus, I conclude that my (current) teaching philosophy, as related to postgraduate teaching, can be stated as: *I wish for my students, the attainment of entrepreneurial knowledge that leads to entrepreneurial wisdom. I want my students to discover themselves in the lives they live. I want my students to be excited about learning and fearless of failing in the same breath. I want my students to be able to create opportunities for satisfaction within and after their university studies.* Sound familiar? It should, it is the exact teaching philosophy espoused in *Teaching Entrepreneurship to Undergraduates*.

So what has changed substantially? Let us revisit the list of reflection questions that were offered for consideration in *Teaching Entrepreneurship to Undergraduates*. First, how do you believe your students learn? In this respect, I identify several important differences between pedagogy and andragogy (see Wlodkowski, 1999). My postgraduate students tend be less dependent upon me if given sufficient guidance. They also tend to contextualise the nature of their learning more readily to their lived life experiences. They tend to be more capable of classroom discussion through which their fellow students in turn gain added value to their own personal learning. They also tend to demonstrate a greater appreciation to the potential value of the knowledge and skills they are developing. Essentially they are generally quick to accept deficits in the knowledge/skills they have to combat the problems they face in life on a daily basis. Therefore, I observe they are more forward thinking in terms of what they will gain immediately from their studies.

Second, the potential impact of their learning is more discernable. While some postgraduate students are drawn back to higher education to complete a personal journey previously missed, many also seem to use it as a means to shift lanes and gears and move forward to a new (or least upgraded) role in society. My students want what adds immediate value and care less for that which doesn't; they are potentially rebooting a career, not building a resume.

Third, my students wish to engage in learning activities that facilitate their capacity to transfer knowledge/skills within the world they currently reside in (Wlodkowski, 1999). Alternatively, my undergraduate students are content to accept the potential *future* application of knowledge/skills to remote or novel contexts that they have yet to encounter.

Fourth, my postgraduate students, many attending university for the first time require a respectful and social space to feel comfortable. A space that naturally connects seamlessly to the lives they are embedded within. A space that is curious about their life learning and supportive of their willingness to express their opinions. Therefore, the learning environment that we would wish for our undergraduate students is an absolute necessity for postgraduate students.

Lastly, assessing the nature of your students learning. To be honest, I observe far less interest in grades than I do in *confidence* by my postgraduate students. If the nature of assessment has enabled the student to feel confident, that is, they have developed a competence vis-à-vis the application of knowledge/skills to problems and opportunities, then my students tend to be satisfied. Alternatively, my undergraduate students need to see assessment outcomes converted into a high grade so as to help build their resume. I sense that grades provide short-term confidence whereas peer and self-assessed proficiency contributes to long-term confidence. Given that confidence is acknowledged to be a key antecedent of entrepreneurial behaviour, this is an import issue to bear in mind. Hopefully, the above discussion demonstrates that when I work in amongst postgraduate students I draw upon different skills and approaches to keep my teaching philosophy alive.

## TEACHING PHILOSOPHIES MORE BROADLY

As previously stated elsewhere (Jones, 2011), it is my intention to provide you the reader with multiple opportunities to reflect on how your teaching philosophy is influencing the learning of your students. As always, I hope you benefit from gaining insights into the approaches of other entrepreneurship educators, whose thoughts are shared here as well. Again, the focus is less about what is being taught, and more concerned with how they are being taught. I recently stumbled across a passage in a book celebrating a series of lectures given at Harvard University by Charles Saunders Peirce in 1898 (Ketner, 1992), in which he is quoted as saying:

> … it is not the man who thinks he knows it all, that can bring other men to feel their need of learning, and it is only a deep sense that one is miserably ignorant that can spur one in the toilsome path of learning. That is why, to my very humble apprehension, it cannot but seem that those admirable pedagogical methods for which the American teacher is distinguished are of little more consequence than the cut of his coat, that they surely are as nothing compared with that fever for learning that must consume the soul of the man who is to infect others with the same apparent malady.

It is difficult to discuss teaching philosophies in any prescriptive or normative sense. I think that in the above quote from Peirce the reason for this is obvious; not only are we as educators a highly diverse lot, so too are our students. In one sense, it makes this chapter easier to write, in another sense, more difficult. For its not within the hidden depths of our pedagogical or andragogical talents that our worth is to be found; as we already know that good teaching cannot be reduced to technique (Palmer, 1997). Rather, it is the very essence of who we are and how we connect to the various types of students we interact with that matters most. It is through such interaction that our humility is sharpened. It is here that our absolute inability to be all things to all people is brought clearly into focus.

There is a sense of continuous pleasure gained from meeting EE educators and peering into their psyche. Looking for clues as to what sort of *fever* they seek to spread amongst their cohorts. Whilst we cannot claim to hold any mortgage on such a disposition, I feel confident from my meanderings around EE conferences that EE educators would seem to be inflicted at a higher than average rate of such *fever*. It is what sets us apart from the well-drilled business school educator; it is what gets us into strife quite frequently; it is what makes all the difference in our students learning and self-development. Given the obvious importance of this issue, and the feedback I have received since *Teaching Entrepreneurship to Undergraduates*, I thought it appropriate to address this in considerably more detail. Further, I wish for the remainder of this chapter to provide an overarching framework from where your thinking across the other chapters can be collated, contemplated, and acted-upon. To this end, I will introduce the idea of pedagogical content knowledge (Shulman, 1986) with the aim of broadening your appreciation of the integrated mechanics of one's teaching philosophy and teaching practice.

## PEDAGOGICAL CONTENT KNOWLEDGE

The issue of course content is inextricably related to the orientation of the educator. Have you ever reflected deeply upon the roots of your explanations, the focus of your teaching, your understanding of your students' learning and/or your ability to help them develop confidence in their abilities? Let us go one step further. Reflect upon the analogies, metaphors and other stories you use to convey meaning. Are they borrowed from elsewhere or born from the circumstances of your life? Unless your teaching practice has been from within a vacuum, there is very likely to be an inherent predisposition, developed from your various life experiences, that orients you towards certain teaching practices and away from other practices.

Consider yourself as a learner; are you a mirror of that learner as a teacher? That many of us are should not be overly surprising. As Parker Palmer has stated, 'we teach who we are' (1997: 7). Therefore, in this section I invite you to revisit your roots to better appreciate your predispositions so as to enable you to gather your bearings. First, lets be clear of the direction I am inviting your thinking to follow. I wish for you to consider who you are as a person, a learner and as a teacher. Following this I will encourage you to finds links between yourself and the content knowledge you hold germane to EE. In terms of understanding the interrelations between yourself, the content focus provided by you to your learners, I aim for you to discover your pedagogical content knowledge (PCK) position. That is your specific knowledge of what and how to teach specific content to mature students of entrepreneurship.

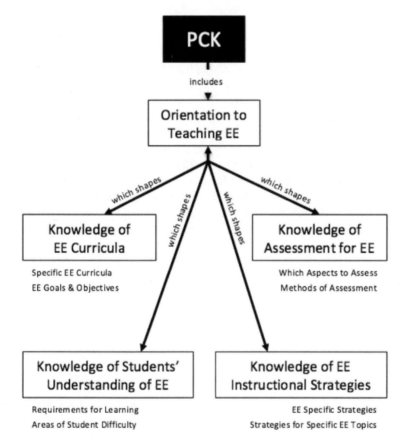

**Adapted from:** Magnusson, Krajcik and Borko (1999)

*Figure 1.1 Components of PCK for EE teaching*

I believe the conceptualisation of PCK by Magnusson et al (1999), as illustrated in Figure 1.1, is simple and applicable to EE. This framework accounts for the educators' orientation towards teaching EE, their knowledge and beliefs about EE curriculum, their knowledge and beliefs about students' understanding of EE topics, their knowledge and beliefs about assessment of EE, and their knowledge and belief of instructional strategies for EE. A brief discussion of these five elements will reaffirm their value to your thinking. These five elements will be revisited in the final chapter to offer you an opportunity to gather your thinking into a framework for on going future development.

**Your Orientation to Teaching**

How might your account for your teaching orientation? What knowledge and beliefs do you hold regarding the development of and provision of EE? The answers to such deep questions lay deep beneath the surface of what is offered to your students at first contact. Personally, I have descended from Native American Indian heritage. I am increasingly aware of the importance of the medicine wheel in their culture and more specifically, their approach to education (see Klug and Whitfield, 2003). I take from my ancestors a constant consideration for balancing what I know (my intuition), what I dream (my illuminations), what I reflect upon (my introspective nature) and what I must test (my innocence). As I develop as an educator, I increasingly sense that my orientation to teaching EE is a property of my past, present and immediate future. I take confidence in my abilities to find this balance and to share this disposition with my students so that they also understand my thinking. So, in terms of this first element of the PCK framework, from where does your orientation come? What is buried deep within you? How might you explain your internal compass to your students?

**Knowledge of EE Curriculum**

It is always interesting to discuss the goals and objectives EE educators hold. Clearly context matters a great deal (see Penaluna, Penaluna and Jones, 2012) in the development and delivery of EE. Broadly speaking we tend to be split loosely into a two camps. There are those that educate more so to develop the enterprising mindset, and there are those that employ a greater focus on the business start-up process. The context of the curriculum will typically influence one's position along this imaginary continuum. I say imaginary because in reality it is quite likely you cannot achieve a focus on the latter without due consideration of the former. In my experience, the work of Nigel Adams at the University of Buckingham in the UK achieves such a balance.

Nigel's students *all* enrol with an explicit focus on starting a viable business. In reality, such an explicit outcome is not common for students of EE; therefore, such a balance can be difficult to achieve. Too often we have too little curriculum time with our students to adequately enable them to traverse this imaginary continuum. Thus, your ability to state what are your goals and objectives is of critical importance. How does your approach and knowledge of it conform to, or perhaps inform local, state, national or global EE policy? The recent work of Andy Penaluna (see QAA, 2012) highlights the importance of being able to define with clarity the role and purpose of entrepreneurship and enterprise education in the UK context.

Clearly you need to be able to stake out and defend your territory. Why do you have your goals and objectives? From what context have they been developed, borrowed or co-developed? To what extent do you communicate to all stakeholders your knowledge of EE and its various curriculums? Lastly, and most importantly, how does this knowledge feedback into your *current* orientation to teaching EE?

**Knowledge of Assessment in EE**

From your determination, what specific aspects of EE can be and should be assessed? In my experience, the high frequency of experiential education methods leads to suspicion and concern amongst other educators who teach alongside us in related areas. Your ability to hold knowledge of EE, and specifically what should be assessed and how it should (or could) be assessed is critical. Very few educators in our field have paid sufficient attention to the issue of assessment, although see the impressive work of Luke Pittaway (Pittaway and Edwards, 2012; Pittaway, Hannon, Gibb and Thompson, 2009).

In *Teaching Entrepreneurship to Undergraduates*, Allan Gibb identified 44 different teaching pedagogies used for EE. That clearly represents potentially an enormous array of assessment methods also being used in EE. To what extent are you aware of what is being used and why such methods are favoured over other potential methods? Are you able to articulate the advantages and disadvantages related to using any particular assessment method or technique? Given the experiential nature of much EE, it is important that we collectively contribute to a growing body of knowledge as to what methods of assessment are appropriate for EE. Again, your knowledge related to this element of the PCK framework will also most likely feedback into your overall orientation to teaching.

**Knowledge of Students' Understanding of EE**

This element of the PCK framework relates to what knowledge or beliefs you hold as to any prerequisite knowledge or skills for learning about/for/or through EE. Clearly, the position you hold regarding your goals and objectives will shape your opinions here. For example, if you hold a stronger focus on developing an enterprising mindset then you may place less emphasis upon students arriving with solid knowledge of the principles of accounting, finance, marketing and economics. However, if your focus is upon the actual start-up process, the opposite requirement may be the case.

For many students, topics such as failure, risk taking and the absence of regular income are very difficult to comprehend and therefore learn about. Understanding which issues certain types of adult learners may struggle with is also very important. We simply cannot assume that each student can move from the first topic area to the last with the same degree of ease. For example, just merely conceptualising the role of the entrepreneur in society is very challenging for many students. As we will discuss in the next chapter, we are the products of our lives and our students come to us with significant diversity of life experiences. Your ability to comprehend such differences is central to your ability to construct learning opportunities that cater to the diversity of your student cohorts. Again, your orientation to teaching will most likely alter as you recognise the degrees of understanding your students' hold towards EE. The last element of the PCK framework deals with the issue of instructional strategies.

**Knowledge of EE Instructional Strategies**

Typically, your knowledge in this area can be organised around your EE (or subject) specific knowledge and also your knowledge of topic specific strategies. It would be expected that your (preferred) knowledge of subject specific knowledge would significantly influence your orientation to teaching EE. Personally, I focus upon the personal development of each student prior to focussing upon the development of their ideas. Other colleagues approach their teaching from the opposite direction and some find a middle ground approach that doesn't overtly over-emphasise either end of this imaginary continuum.

It was observed in *Teaching Entrepreneurship to Undergraduates* that the sources of influence for educator orientations to teaching vary wildly. Only a few luminaries (such as Gibb, Bygrave or Kuratko) were noted as directly influencing the approach of the educators surveyed. In other words, what we know of our subject area tends to be quite personal and developed from the close surrounds we work in. This has the potential advantage of educators being able to co-evolve their teaching practice alongside the needs of their students and institutions. Alternatively, it may mean that EE educators may perhaps be quite ignorant of other good practices in our field. Whichever the case, it is important that we are alert to what practices exist beyond our own horizons. The excellent handbooks of Fayolle (2007a; 2007b; 2010) provide wonderful insights into the teaching orientations and practices of EE educators the world over. The question arises, to what extent can we really claim to know and understand the orientations and practices of our fellow educators? Is the diversity of our practices working for us or against us?

In terms of topic specific strategies, there are different levels of weighting given to specific topics in our teaching. For example, I place less emphasis upon the importance of writing a business plan than I do on knowing how to read a business plan; many other educators do the reverse. However, in my experience, the most important aspect here is our abilities to invent new representations of the topics we determine offer potential value to our students' learning. In this sense, the experience of the educator as an entrepreneur comes to the fore, with stories, analogies and models quite often developed in such a way as to gain traction within the minds of our students.

Further, as educators with entrepreneurial experience we often seem to have unique insights that enable us to develop innovative activities through which deep experiential learning is possible. There appears (relative to other areas of education) a genuine desire to allow our students to experiment with their learning. Personally, I feel this makes sense when you factor in the diversity of learning styles present within a typical cohort. Rather than assuming a topic can be learnt in a particular way, inviting non-conforming expressions of interest from our learners makes perfect sense. To conclude, what do you know of instructional practices in our field? To what extent have you considered how your personal experiences have created biases and/or strengths in your approach to teaching? For the final time, I again state that where you are placed regarding this final element of PCK will of course affect your overall orientation to teaching.

## GLOBAL PERSPECTIVES

Just as in *Teaching Entrepreneurship to Undergraduates*, comment on a range of issues related teaching entrepreneurship to postgraduate students was sought. I will refer to this survey as the IE-II survey in subsequent chapters and details of the survey can be located in Appendix 1. As expected, there was some disagreement as to whether one's teaching philosophy should change between teaching undergraduates and postgraduates. Perhaps this also demonstrates the difficulty in separating one's stated orientation to teaching and one's actual practice of teaching.

As I have stated, I personally hold the same teaching philosophy statement across both levels, but I enact that philosophy in different ways to achieve my desired outcomes vis-à-vis my students' learning. An approach not inconsistent with Aimee Zhang at the University of Wollongong in Australia who saw the need for designing different programs for different students with different background knowledge. However, Dr Jane Nolan at the University of Cambridge in England argues that postgraduates are at a different place in their lives. Undergraduates are sometimes still trying to work out the point and may not engage as well; thus it's even more important to have strategies for engaging them through interactive approaches. Or, as Dr Alicia Castillo, an entrepreneur and invited lecturer at the University of Western Australia feels, postgraduates are more mature and have more life experiences to reflect upon, they also have more responsibilities, so curriculum changes have to be more practical. Thus, given that they have probably heard many of the topics somewhere before, Janice Gates at the Western Illinois University in America sees the need to give more concrete examples or bring up situations that they can apply their learning towards.

While some respondents felt there was little change in their teaching philosophy or practical approach, they tended not to explain the basis of such opinion. As such, at this point in time it might be best to simply acknowledge that such difference of opinion exists. The remaining chapters aim to demonstrate that there is indeed a significant difference and that we educators in our field must address this to aid our students' learning in both domains of study.

## THE DEVELOPMENT OF AN IMPORTANT TOOL

As we move towards a discussion of adults as learners and/or their unique situational issues, be mindful that the ideas presented here aim to be thought provoking. The discussion also will pause occasionally to blend in the thoughts of EE educators from around the world. I hope that you, having progressed this far will travel the remainder of the journey through the pages with your students by your side. The purpose of this book is to further awaken you to your most important tool as an educator; that is you yourself. You are your most important tool. It is you and your scholarship of teaching and learning (see Hutchings, Huber and Ciccone, 2011) which will contribute most to your students' capacity to engage with EE in ways that transforms their lives.

The logic flows a little like this. You are surrounded by numerous interactions. Interactions between you and your students, them between themselves, them between their lives and both them and you and the learning environments you co-create. As discussed in *Teaching Entrepreneurship to Undergraduates*, this range of dialogic relations are not explainable without direct reference to all the pairs of interacting entities. Interactions, which are often largely invisible, yet potentially manageable by the skilful educator. Your ability to develop your PCK will strengthen the nature of your orientation to teaching, which in turn has potential benefits to your current and subsequent students. My own personal contexts serve only as examples, not exemplars. The comments of our fellow educators are presented to restore balance, not lead. The reflection space provide at the conclusion of each chapter provides an opportunity for you to contemplate the nature of interaction you experience, shape, and guide with your students.

# 2. Nascent Entrepreneurship and Adults

The art of teaching is the art of assisting discovery. (Mark Van Doren)

When we step up to engage our adult learners what is our purpose and how might it differ from engaging adolescents? The aim of this chapter is to consider the nature of adults learning about, for or through entrepreneurship. To consider what they uniquely bring to the process of learning and what they might be seeking to gain from the process. Central to such consideration is accounting for the many forms of motivations of our students. Developing this initial focus will hopefully enable the underlying aim of determining how we can assist our students to discover themselves and the nature of the environs they inhabit.

When viewed as social change, entrepreneurship becomes in one sense a simplified phenomenon in society and also in another sense a complex of hundreds of processes and events in society. As with all learning contexts constructed around entrepreneurship we must be careful not to conflate nascent entrepreneurship with learning about entrepreneurship. However, in the case of adult learners, another dimension needs to be factored in. We need to account for the current and future capacity to act, as change agents in the social situations are students are already embedded in.

## THE ADULT LEARNER

The issue of student diversity was addressed in *Teaching Entrepreneurship to Undergraduates* (Jones, 2011) because of its obvious importance. However, in the context of postgraduate studies, this issue takes on additional dimensions (Brookfield, 1986). Our students' abilities as learners have been shaped (both positively and negatively) by their life experiences. In one sense they might be less plastic in the malleable sense, alternatively, they may also be potentially more focused and appreciative of the value of further educating themselves. Our challenge is to ensure they fully understand the potential value of EE, that they are able to see its application to their life so as to ensure sufficient motivation surfaces. Without such true motivation we have students merely learning *about* entrepreneurship, but not necessarily learning *for* and/or *through* entrepreneurship. Whereas the undergraduate student is typically distracted with a concern for starting a career, the postgraduate is *in situ* vis-à-vis their life's journey. So our capacity as educators to unearth intrinsic motivation should be higher with postgrad students than with undergrads, as long as we enable each student to personalise the educational experience.

One of the unique issues about postgraduate EE is that we are more likely to encounter current and nascent entrepreneurs compared to undergraduate education. This paradox here is very ironic. The vast majority of students of entrepreneurship education are undergraduates who are assumed to be the entrepreneurs of tomorrow. The remaining minority are postgraduates (frequently studying in MBA streams) largely assumed capable of becoming better managers. If only we could rid ourselves of the start-up focus we might be able to see the forest for the trees. Within the lives of our postgraduate students lay so much rich entrepreneurial experience. So many of them already have being change agents in society. We risk missing out on everything they have to offer our educational environs by assuming they are merely students of entrepreneurship.

## THE POSTGRADUATE JOURNEY

The real voyage of discovery consists not in seeking new landscapes but in having new eyes. (Marcel Proust)

Consider a series of lines whose intersection represents a point in time. Consider those lines as representing our students' awareness, confidence, motivation and sense of stability. As educators, we can place ourselves at those intersections; we can replace darkness with lightness, fear with confidence, ignorance with awareness and instability with stability. But we cannot place every student on the same intersection; for their different life journeys have been travelled on different roads. They each have an intersection that represents their personal histories. Our job is not to help them create a roadmap. Rather, our purpose is to enable them to understand the roads they have travelled, the wisdom they have collected along the way, and to help them understand how they can move forward from where they are situated.

This is the postgraduate opportunity, as I see it. The transformation in their lives is as much a spiritual and intellectual journey as it is a physical journey. Indeed, the very reason many have not seriously sought to travel an entrepreneurial journey previously is that they have lacked sufficient balance in their ability to learn. There is a need to be able to 'gather the facts of life' and to be 'able to transcend and transform them' (Hart, 2001: 12). In my experience, this journey is potentially too challenging (or too premature) for our undergraduate students, and it is typically overdue and most welcomed by postgraduate students. So long as it does not disrupt the fabric of their current lives.

The ideas of Hart (2001) provide a fascinating outline of how we can assist our students to move from interacting with information, to discerning patterns of knowledge, developing intelligence, demonstrating understanding, and finally, applying wisdom. My experience is that we can develop curricula through which student transformation is possible. That learning can be the journey rather than a means to an end. Once our students can transcend the facts of their lives they potentially present themselves as societal change agents. Exciting, isn't it? I recently asked several cohorts of postgraduate students whom I assisted in their study of entrepreneurship, about any changes in their attitude, confidence or desire to behave entrepreneurially.

> I am more aware of what is going on around me ... I see the gaps. Mind you, I'm not always tempted to fill them ... I just see them! I know I can do anything that I put my mind to and recognise that I can draw on the resources I require from around me. I am not afraid to ask and I don't take it personally if I am rejected. (student comment no. 1)

> I was recently involved in a community project which failed to develop for several reasons. I used my learning from BAA510 to help me create a structure around the project and recognise then research the opportunities that arose from group discussion. (student comment no. 2)

> I see more value than ever in failing, and growing from failure. I am in a place where I now feel I should take more risks. My confidence is not as fragile as it was earlier in time. I am ready to embarrass myself should my grand ideas fail. (student comment no. 3)

As an educator I am thrilled when I receive such feedback. Especially when it is accompanied by other evidence of entrepreneurial behaviour, which it frequently is. The above comments do not relate to my students having collided with a few well-chosen pieces of information. I take great pride in the depth of learning that has occurred. New capacities to see their world in new ways, new ways in which required resources are identified and located, and new ways in which confidence has been established. Is this not what we wish to create in students of entrepreneurship?

Despite my direct absence from the day-to-day lives of my students, I know I am with them on their journeys. My aim is to win their trust, to inspire them to become comfortable with their world and to see its simplicity. By simplicity, I mean for them to understand how the parts and processes fit together. I wish for them all to appreciate the workings of selection mechanisms working for and against ideas and initiatives in society. For this to be possible, I need to offer them a lens through which the complexity of social change can be reduced to observable (or imaginable) parts. More about such a lens later, but let us consider the nature of my attempts to inspire and win the trust of my students.

Wlodkowski (1999) argues that adult learners must immediately sense relevance and choice in their studies to develop favourable attitudes to their studies. This includes positive feelings towards their educator, the subject, themselves as learners and their ability to successfully apply their learning in meaningful ways. Thus, I always start with a focus on introductions, an explanation of how I hope to help them as adult learners, I ensure all interactions are as authentic as possible and finally, I ensure all different styles of learning are acknowledged as welcome. In short, I work on quickly establishing the perception of a safe and supportive learning environment.

In terms of their own self-perceptions as learners, I seek to ensure any doubts are removed by providing opportunities for the class to appreciate the multiple forms of intelligence (Gardner, 1993) we collective share. In this way, each student is respected as a person first and foremost. Their efforts and abilities to learn are respected and even the most unconfident student is encouraged to see themselves as capable learners. This is typically quite easy once attention is given to the task. Our adult learners have all achieved much from the numerous problems they have confronted in life.

As a subject area, entrepreneurship initially tends to be poorly understood by many students. Some assume it is starting a business while others assume it is doing business in new and exciting ways. Few come to the study of entrepreneurship without a business-centred perspective. Depending on the background of your students this may not be too problematic. However, if your students have little experience starting up a business, such assumptions can get in the way of them understanding and/or truly seeing themselves as entrepreneurs. I deliberately seek to take business out of the minds of my students and strip entrepreneurship back to social change in society. In reality they are all well qualified to be students of social change as it relates to the world they live and act in. This approach seems to work well in drawing in the students' interest for the subject. Their world will always be more interesting (to them) than mine, as it should be.

To the extent that an entrepreneurial mindset can be developed, then students can feel positively towards their ability to apply their learning in their daily lives. Given the costs associated with being an adult learner, such as time and money, it is important that students gain from the process.

Beyond our educator assessments of their learning, we need to ensure our students are equipped with a capacity of self-evaluation vis-à-vis their ability to apply their learning. That is, we need to understand their motivations.

## UNDERSTANDING MOTIVATIONS

Historically, my students arrive in class with motivations that can be loosely clustered into several categories. As illustrated in Figure 2.1 below, I identify five primary types of motivations across recent cohorts, all of which must be accommodated. While clearly not an exhaustive description of all the possible motivations that may encapsulate my students' presence in the classroom, they act as an example of how their motivations differ.

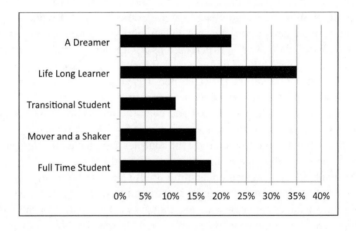

*Figure 2.1    Types of postgraduate motivations at UTAS*

The first type of student I encounter is the dreamer. The dreamer has always longed to break free from the mundane aspects of their life and create something new that demonstrates their latent abilities. Typically, they might be in the middle of their career and a male. Life is passing them by and they hold onto the dream of one day stepping up to create something new. They may be prevented from doing so by the hours they work for someone else or by the time and capital limitations related to their current enterprise activities. Ironically, this type of student is just as likely to be employed or self-employed. Either situation can leave them tied to the responsibilities of their everyday life. Unable to break free and chase that big opportunity that lays hidden away in the recesses of their imagination. They however tend to use

EE as a means to a glorious end, visualising wide-ranging solutions to significant issues.

The second type of student I see is the life-long learner. The life-long learner has a commitment to learning and an innate curiosity about their place is society. From my experience, they may be more likely to be female, underemployed (in terms of hours) but ranging from young to old. Social entrepreneurship has an appeal to the life-long learner, as do activities born from the resources of their lifestyle and hobbies. They like collecting new forms of knowledge, and hold confidence as to the eventual application of such knowledge. Their motivations in our classrooms may however be less than desired as they balance their curiosity across multiple domains of informal and formal learning. They also see as EE as another opportunity to add more tools their never-ending supply of potential tools.

The third student type is the transitional student, a student seeking some breathing space before deciding the next phase of life. EE provides them with a new view of the world, their resource profile (Aldrich and Matinez, 2001) and its development is of most interest. I have found this student to be typically female, and the oldest of my observed student types. They tend to always work, but mostly part-time and demonstrate the most motivation to their studies. Studying EE provides an opportunity to study themselves and the experiences they have collected thus far. They show the most interest in starting their own business, typically to compliment their existing part-time incomes.

The fourth student type is the mover and shaker, the quintessential enterprising soul trapped in a student's body. They tend to be younger, already working long hours and using education to extend their qualifications. Their employment is a means to an end, starting a business is a serious goal. They are motivated by EE and impulsive and keen to contribute in classroom discussion; everything is possible. EE tends to reaffirm their natural confidence and bring forward their planning timelines as they develop a clearer sense of what they are born to achieve.

The fifth and final student type is the full-time student. Not surprisingly they tend to be young, male, working very few hours and quite often international students. EE is but one of several components of a qualification building process. Their focus on EE can be diluted by their simultaneous consideration of other subject areas. EE tends to advantage them in terms of building confidence and opening their minds to alternative career pathways. Their motivations for EE are often driven by a sense of future responsibility to a family run business to which they may help manage upon returning home.

In summary, my understanding of student motivations for EE is possible by seeing subsets of student types who I encounter. They may or may not be the same types you encounter. That doesn't really matter. The key is that you don't assume their motivations are too similar. For once the variance in their motivations is discovered you can play your role in ensuring that your students find interest and meaning in EE as it relates to their life. Let us consider again the views of educators globally with regards the opportunities and challenges postgraduate students of EE face.


## POSTGRADUATE OPPORTUNITIES AND CHALLENGES

Many of the IE-II survey respondents agreed on a range of opportunities and challenges. There was a clear sense of the paradox faced by postgraduate students, seemingly wiser, yet tied to the responsibilities of their lives. Dr Alicia Castillo from the Wealthing Group in Australia felt that it is easier for postgraduates because they can validate assumptions based on their experience. Conversely, it is difficult because they can see how hard it can be, and they usually have commitments that force them to avoid risks. In a similar vein, Monica Kreuger, President of Global Infobrokers in Canada, observed that (in comparison to undergraduates) they have more life experience and therefore larger social and business networks and a larger frame of reference to place the learning. Further, she sensed they are also more bound by past life experience and frequently find it more difficult to step out of the comfort zone. These similar observations form the focus of the following chapter.

One of the other perspectives noted was the challenge faced from having been *shaped* by life itself. Dr Griselda Correa at the Universidad del Turabo in Puerto Rico sensed that adult learners might be contaminated by previous work experience and insights into the tough reality of succeeding as an entrepreneur. Or, as Dr Bill Kirkley at Massey University in New Zealand noted, they often come to study with a fixed mind-set and perspective of how things should be. Katie Wray at Newcastle University in the United Kingdom argues this may be because they have already been more influenced by academia and traditional employment routes.

Whilst such comments demonstrate support for or against postgraduates becoming entrepreneurs, perhaps in hindsight a better question would have focussed upon their capacity to be more entrepreneurial. When challenges and opportunities are considered vis-à-vis postgraduates starting a new business, the opposing views appear quite balanced. However, if we were to isolate our concerns to simply being more entrepreneurial in their current and future roles in society, then the true potential of EE becomes apparent. The obvious experience-based advantages are amplified and the situational challenges seemed largely negated. What seems obvious is that it is we who will or won't prevent our students' lives from getting in the way of their learning.

## CONNECTING OUR STUDENTS TO THEIR LEARNING

Our students assemble before us as individuals who have walked radically differently lives. They have experienced different personal and societal upbringings, inherited or adopted different values, been luckier or unluckier than each other, and accumulated different degrees of knowledge and expertise in diverse areas of society. Acknowledging the diversity of our students' motivations and life experiences requires the EE educator to ensure that this diversity is the primary organising factor, not merely something that is easily lost within a list of student identification numbers. Brookfield (1990) states the role of learning communities are critical in enabling adults to survive and indeed flourish in study environments. We are not their most important learning resource; they collectively hold the most potential to aid each other's learning.

Cultivating an environment where like-minded students can identify with each other and feel comfortable to develop friendships is very important. Being entrepreneurial does not require one to start at A and progress to B. It takes courage, it takes initiative, and it requires a great deal of social interaction. Many of our students may hold many of the attributes required to succeed in their entrepreneurial efforts, but just lack the confidence within them to initiate the first steps. Despite the leadership they display in other aspects of their lives and their ability to confidently know and use closely related knowledge, EE students are frequently intimidated by the thought of being entrepreneurial. As educators we can lead them towards the formation of learning communities that have the potential to remain productive long beyond our active involvement.

At this point in time you might be feeling a little redundant, that your role as an educator is being downsized. In their seminal paper titled *Many are Called, but Few are Chosen*, Aldrich and Martinez (2001) capture the numerical challenge that haunts the process of entrepreneurship. We need considerably more trying in order to get a sufficient number succeeding. And so it is with our students. We need them all attempting to conceive, create and capture new value in order to ensure the actual value to society of EE is realised. We don't have the luxury of guaranteeing entrepreneurial success upon graduation. We do however have the ability to ensure everyone has the opportunity to walk someway in the shoes of the entrepreneur (Gibb, 2002). In this sense, the challenge of the educator is to focus on the learning process possible for each individual student, rather than merely focusing upon the delivery of their own solo performance.

The argument being made is that to connect our students to their learning we need to recognise the ever-present diversity that surrounds each cohort and to use it to our advantage. If our teaching practice is shaped by recognition of such diversity we inevitably draw upon our own diverse set of approaches, employ a greater variety of interactive techniques and encourage multiple communication formats. Brookfield (1990) argues that in doing so we are more likely to achieve two things. First, we increase the chances of enabling our students to engage in ways that best work for them. Second, we increase to the opportunities for our students to experience learning in new and exciting ways that further challenge them as learners.

As our students move from an orientation to the *subject of* entrepreneurship to seeing *learning to be* entrepreneurial they potentially engage in emancipatory learning (Cranton, 1994). This I believe is the ultimate goal of EE, the emancipation of individual students from the roadblocks and lack of self-belief that all too often beset their lives. As we dare to contemplate such a wonderful education landscape, we must also be honest about the role required of us to support our students in such a manner. Aronsson (2004) in his interview with David Birch identifies the common approach to EE in most business school. An approach that is compatible with most other faculties; teach students the knowledge and skills required to become good employees. Herein lies our greatest challenge, being entrepreneurial educators within a system that typically reinforces the opposite.


## FROM PEDAGOGY TO ANDRAGOGY

This chapter will conclude by providing you with some space to reflect upon your current approach to teaching entrepreneurship to postgraduate students, perhaps as contrasted to your approach to undergraduates. Knowles (1980) provides an insightful comparison of such differences. From a pedagogical approach the learner is highly dependent upon the educator, with the educator determining what is to be learned, how it is to be learned, when it is to be learned and indeed, if it already has been learned. In contrast, from an andragogical approach a greater degree of self-directedness is expected with the educator nurturing and guiding their learning to an area of their choosing. How does this contrast play out in your world? Are you playing different roles, or does your dominant role in the undergraduate world spill over into the postgraduate world? If so, what are the consequences for your students' learning and what can you do to address this?

If we now turn to your consideration of the students' experience, does your practice differ across both types of students? From a pedagogical perspective we typically see the student as the empty vessel to be built upon. Commonly lectures with powerpoints and audio-visuals are used to transfer information. Alternatively, from an andragogical approach we aim to tap into the reservoir of experience and knowledge that has already been developed. We aim to leverage such accumulation to contextualise their learning; thus we aim to use more experiential and hands on approaches. Does this ring true for you approach? Are your postgraduates treated with respect and allowed to bring with them their accumulated knowledge and experience as their tools of learning in your classroom? If not, do you think their ability to maximise their learning opportunities are being lessened?

Have you spent time thinking about your students' readiness to learn? We take for granted that our relatively homogeneous undergraduates are ready to learn and that they will benefit from exposure to a fairly standardised curriculum. However, as demonstrated in the above discussion, we meet our postgraduate students at different times in their lives as they deal with the different circumstances of their lives. From an andragogical perspective we should be seeking to help them solve the problems and/or exploit the opportunities in their lives by ensuring they solve the issues they need to address. Clearly, we are working with a heterogeneous group of students at the postgraduate level. Does your approach accommodate such individual curiosity?

Lastly, are your students learning to build a CV? Are they seeking to acquire knowledge and skills for future application? Or, are they seeking to shift gears and changes lanes? Perhaps seeking to become more effective and efficient with the problems and opportunities that sit currently in their actual lives. How do you span this pedagogical-andragogical divide? Do you practice your craft differently in each domain? The remainder of this book will hopefully reinforce the need to do so and provide you with ideas in how to think about the challenges in your own teaching world. The next chapter takes us into the world of our postgraduate students and contemplates what the process of learning could be like for students of EE.

# 3.   The Situational Dilemma

The question is not whether transformation happens: it does. We change and grow. Instead, the question is whether we can help transformation along. Can we create an education that invites, even nudges transformation? (Hart, 2001: 13)

Having discussed the diversity of knowledge and experience our postgraduate students bring with them, our attention now turns to exploiting such diversity to the benefit of our students. On the front cover of this book is an illustration of lizards. The sex-determining mechanisms observed in many lizards alter depending upon the environments the female lizards encounter (Pen, Uller, Feldmeyer, Harts, While and Wapstra, 2010). That is, colder or warmer climates will directly influence the distribution of male and female lizards born in a given population. Rather than assuming genetic inheritance will comprehensively explain sex-determining mechanisms, the role of environmentally induced change must also be factored in.

As strange as this chapter introduction may seem, the aim is to construct a framework for you to envisage yourself as the architect of an environment that aids transformational learning. To achieve this, it is necessary to discuss the mechanics of the processes required. It is important that the basics of the mechanics are understood in an abstract way so that you can imagine their operation in your world. Think of your students as crossing a threshold when they interact with you and your fellow students, like the lizards on the front cover. Think of them as being altered in the way they see and react to their environs. Think of yourself as being the architect of creating a process of selection and personal space for your students to experience behavioural change. As Dewey (1933: 22) observed, 'we never educate directly, but indirectly by means of the environment. Whether we permit chance environments to do the work, or whether we design environments for the purpose makes a great difference'. Note, here I am using behavioural change in its broadest sense to include feeling, thinking as well as overt action (Tyler, 1949). Before we further consider the role of diversity let us consider the transformative process being contemplated.

# STUDENT PLASTICITY

The development of the individual in society has been studied for many years. Crudely, we as individuals inherit a genetic code that sets us on a particular developmental journey, aspects of which may be modified positively or negatively as we encounter different environments across our lives. At the close of the nineteenth century, James Baldwin (1896) proposed a new factor in evolution, subsequently referred to as the Baldwin effect. Amongst other processes, he proposed that beneficial (psycho-genetic) traits could be expected to be supportive of ontogenetic plasticity. He suggested that individuals able to acquire traits aligned to the demands of their current and future environs via trial-and-error learning, instruction, conscious intelligence and/or imitation would become better adapted than those that could not.

Roll forward a hundred or so years and the issue of brain plasticity is a hot topic. The brain's ability to be altered and adapt as a result of personal experience is now also a concern for adult development as well. Michael Merzenich (2009) argues that 'our individual skills and abilities are very much shaped by our environments, and that environment extends into our contemporary culture, the thing our brains are challenged with. Because what we have done in our personal evolutions is build up a large repertoire of specific skills and abilities' that are all derived from our brains' plasticity. From this perspective, we are all constructed from the billions of events we individually experience through our lives. As educators, we have the privilege to create environments that herald in new experiences and events into our students' lives. We have the power to shape our students' interactions with enterprise, to foster it, support it and encourage it.

The famous economist Thorsten Veblen (1922: 193) once said 'if any portion or class of society is sheltered from the action of the environment in any essential respect, that portion of the community, or that class, will adapt its views and its scheme of life more tardily to the altered general situation'. He also noted that 'freedom and facility of readjustment ... depends in great measure on the degree of freedom ... [and] ... the degree of exposure of the individual members to the constraining forces of the environment'. Buried within this sage wisdom, I argue, lies our hidden responsibility as educators. Students of EE need the opportunity to adjust to the requirements of new and challenging environments. Thus, we need to see our role as the architects of challenging environments. We need to vacate the central or dominant traditional role educators play in our students' lives and provide the space for them to step up.

Recent studies have demonstrated that certain factors must be present to optimise the process of adult learning (Thomas, 2012). We must ensure that the challenges we engineer for our students provide a degree of difficulty beyond that of the students' current abilities. We also need to ensure that the challenge presented provides an appropriate motivational state. Lastly, we need to ensure that appropriate forms of feedback exist to guide the students' development. On top of this, there must be the availability of *general benefits* to the student. I argue that in EE the actual situation of each student can be brought to life to double as a stage upon which general benefits can be pursued. To the extent that genuine excitement can be garnered within our students to learn how to solve problems or take advantage of opportunities in their lives, structural brakes (Bavelier, Levi, Li, Dan and Hensch, 2010) that reduce plasticity over one's life can be released somewhat.

To summarise, if we are to contribute to the development of transformative learning within our students we must fully appreciate our role as the architects of challenging environments. We must situate the learning process within the individual lives of our students to ensure the perception of genuine benefits exists. We must ensure each student is sufficiently challenged so that they are stretched beyond their existing mental and skill endowments. We must also ensure that learning is the link between their current state and a desired future state. Finally we must provide formative and summative forms of assessment to support the gradual process of change within each student. To the extent that you can create such specific mechanisms of selection and personal space for your students to experience behavioural change, you and your students will most likely benefit. Having briefly discussed the notion of student plasticity, we can return to the issue of diversity that I argue ultimately underwrites our abilities as educators in this space to sink or swim.

## USING STUDENT DIVERSITY

Past studies considering the value and role of diversity in education settings has tended to focus on socio-economic and/or multicultural factors. Hornak and Oritz (2004: 91) have reported that leveraging ever-present diversity can lead to students broadening their worldviews, developing the capacity to critically examine society and being able 'enter high-risk situations with more confidence'. From my experience the values of exploiting diversity within the learning processes in EE also leads to similar outcomes. When we act as the knowledge holder, the main actor in the room, we ignore the unlimited contributions of our students. Worse still, we restrict their learning by denying them an opportunity to learn from each other.

Whilst on one hand we need to surface the life experiences from our students to aid their learning, we also need to enable them to internalise the rich experiences of others. In a typical class I will have a majority of students who have already behaved entrepreneurially. It is my responsibility to use these authentic experiences to help my students learn about change that is already happening in their communities. The process through which this process occurs will be outlined in full detail in chapter eight. Until then, the focus will remain upon harnessing the diversity of our students' life experiences. Let us consider the opinions of how other educators see this issue playing out in their world.

**Global Perspectives**

There appears to be strong support from educators around the globe for proactively using the diversity of our postgraduate students to aid their learning. Although it must be noted that many educators noted a clear distinction between mature age postgraduates and recently graduated undergraduates becoming postgraduates. In terms of the previously stated focus of the book, mature adult learners, the following comments relate to this type of postgraduates.

Many of the IE-II survey respondents echoed each other's thoughts. Dr Wanida Wadeecharoen of Thonburi University in Thailand noted the importance of sharing experiences using group discussions. Extending this point, the importance of ensuring students are fully engaged in their thinking during such discussion was identified by Aimee Zhang at the University of Wollongong in Australia. Complementing such commonly held views was the observation by Professor David Rae of Lincoln University in the UK, that such processes should start with reflection and awareness of such experiences. What these responses demonstrate is the simple and practical ways in which educators seek to draw out the diversity of experiences that too often remain dormant in postgraduate students.

Peter Balan of the University of South Australia in Australia feels that he can challenge postgraduate students more when it comes to identifying possible implementation methods. He observes that he can also challenge postgraduate students to reflect on and discuss the *reasonableness* of possible courses of action, whereas undergraduates have much more limited work and life experience. Dr Kirk Heriot of Columbus State University in the USA, noted that postgraduate students can relate to processes and the implementation of theory in a practical setting. Again this is a common theme amongst respondents. Experience matters and it has a special form currency for EE students.

In addition to this, experience is born from both past success and failure. Dr Jane Nolan at the University of Cambridge in the UK felt that failure and/or making mistakes is an important way of learning. Their life experience may make them more able to acknowledge that we don't always get things right and that we can learn valuable lessons from that life experience. The flip side being that whilst the going is often tough, the prize is having choices and having ownership of your own goals. This is a nice observation; it identifies that issue of tradeoffs that exist in our students' lives. Such tradeoffs clearly vary from student in line with their motivations.

Monica Kreuger of Global Infobrokers in Canada captures these related ideas, suggesting we should always ask our students contextualise their learning into their past experiences, use their connections to develop ideas/applications or conduct research, identify problems and solutions in the *real* world based upon their life experience. She also argues that their learning should be continually ground back into their reality and blended through the realities of their fellow students via collaborative learning. Such sentiments relate nicely to the thoughts of Geraldine McGing of Griffith College in Ireland who argues for peer-centred learning, group problem solving with the lecturer not being the primary knowledge holder. Katie Wray at the Newcastle University in the United Kingdom extends this thinking further arguing for the use of collaborative mentoring, encouraging students to bring their own case studies into class to use as authentic inputs for problem-based learning. It would seem that based on the respondents contributions, there are many forms of andragogical practice consistent with that deliberately aim to exploit student diversity. Let us now consider the voice of the student in this respect.

## LISTENING TO OUR STUDENTS

Now is the appropriate time to introduce the voice of my students, to see what contributions to this discussion they can make. First, the issue of the students' situation will be considered. What is evident in the comments below is that whilst the students outline different constraints they also illustrate different types and degrees of motivation.

> My situation as an adult learner has had an extreme influence - I have a young family and therefore need to have job security to pay the bills - hence my second job as an outlet and channel for my entrepreneurial inclinations. If I was younger and without dependents, I would probably take more risks, calculated, of course. (student comment no. 1)

> Becoming a Grandmother at 43 has been a gift and a shock. It has got me thinking about how can I make a bigger difference for the next generation that will make things better. My extensive experiences and ideas need to be explored more. (student comment no. 2)

It is fair to say I have stayed on the path most travelled most of my life but I find now that I look for the side road that presents opportunities and challenges. I have always been afraid of failure. I have learned that this is sometimes a necessary part of the process and a valuable learning path. (student comment no. 3)

I am very well supported by family, which has enabled me to return to study with a young family. It also allows me to follow my own dreams/path and see where it takes me. (student comment no. 4)

I have owned and operated four enterprises over a period of 30 years. Some more successful than others, but all learning experiences. These studies have re-energized me to get back to doing what I want for me. (student comment no. 5)

I have two children, a husband, and a need to pay ever-increasing bills. I sometimes feel completely trapped by my life situation, but I do not feel negative about it. I adore my family. But I do have itchy feet, and a desire to *do*. I know the time will be right at some stage in the future for me to bounce forward. If only my conscience would back off sometimes and stop telling me I am the *carer*. (student comment no. 6)

Within the above selection of comments my past students reveal their unique situational challenges. They have roles within their families and society that cannot be easily ignored. Their lives have stability that they wish not to disrupt. They are getting older and thinking about their energy levels and the security required in retirement. They contemplate the legacy they may provide to future generations. They are mindful of the obligations they owe to their families and communities. If we contemplate the situations our undergraduate students are derived from we see less constraints and more (perhaps naïve) expectations of what the future might become. In contrast, our postgraduates are a reflection of the current status of their lives; their futures must also factor in the reality of their actual situations. In light of this, let us briefly consider the nature of any transformation within my postgraduate students.

Yes, I am more aware of what is going on around me; I see the gaps. Mind you, I'm not always tempted to fill them; I just see them! I know that I can do anything that I put my mind to and recognize that I can draw what resources I require from around me. I am not afraid to ask and I don't take it personally if I am rejected. (student comment no. 7)

I am now more confident as I can understand the theory in relation to the way I've always instinctively operated as an entrepreneur. (student comment no. 8)

I have much more understanding of what it takes to be an entrepreneur. I have more confidence in my abilities as an intrapreneur and have seen some good results in my workplace as a result. (student comment no. 9)

Yes. I see more value than ever in failing, and growing from failure. I am in a place where I now feel I *should* take more risks. My confidence is not as fragile as it was earlier in time. I am ready to embarrass myself should my grand ideas fail. (student comment no. 10)

What is evident in these few comments is the increased confidence that is driving the students towards new forms of behaviour. Different degrees of perception, making connections between abstract ideas and reality, overcoming fears and gaining a sense of motivation all constitute new behaviours for many students. When the notion of brain plasticity is being discussed, this is ultimately what is the end product.

I believe what is occurring here to be a form of emancipatory learning (Cranton, 1994: 16), or 'a process of freeing ourselves from forces that limit our options and our control over our lives, forces that have been taken for granted or seen as beyond our control'. This is a very important point, in contrast to our undergraduates who arrive like new putty; our postgraduates frequently arrive quite set in their ways. It is our challenge to deepen the awareness our students hold of their surrounds (Freire, 1974) so that the forces that shape their lives can be better seen and understood. In chapter eight, the notion of avoidable and unavoidable bad luck will be discussed in detail. For now however, this idea will be used to demonstrate a simple logic.

Our students live their lives unaware of all the forces and factors that may come to shape their lives positively or negatively. Despite their confidence or cautiousness there can be no direct relationship assumed between their purpose and the consequence of their eventual actions. Sumner (1902: 67) argues beautifully that 'motives and purposes are in the brain and heart of man. Consequences are in the world of fact. The former are infected by human ignorance, folly, self-deception, and passion; the latter are sequences of cause and effect dependent upon the nature of the forces at work'. To free our students from their ignorance the true state of their situated lives must become apparent to *them*. For we as educators cannot know of the factors and forces at play in their lives; there exists no textbook with such information.

In the aftermath of action, reflections can be made as to why particular consequences have occurred. In the ignorance of the factors and forces at play that have shaped the consequences the success or otherwise of our initial motives and/or purposes can always be explained humbly with reference to luck. For now, let us consider the case of undesired consequences. How often do we hear and explanation of undesired consequences based upon bad luck? Clearly if you are unaware of the factors and forces that will determine the eventual consequences bad luck will always stand a strong chance of being drafted in as the culprit.

However, let's assume that the process of EE has led students towards a new ability to discern their surroundings with greater precision. In ways that enable them to play their motives and purposes forward in time, well beyond their earlier mental endowments. All of a sudden, a raft of potential factors and forces that await naïve action are made visible. Actual risk now enters the equation and judgments become informed. In chapter ten, the underlying processes related to the development of such mental agility will be discussed. For now, the issue is one of understanding your role as an educator in endowing your students with a gift that keeps on giving.

## THE EDUCATOR AND THE SITUATED STUDENT

We need to start this discussion with a big question. Do you want to be the architect of a learning environment designed to support emancipatory learning? Hopefully by now the case is solidly developing for thinking about your students' learning on an individual basis. That is, rather than seeing your students moving collectively from point A to point B, you are factoring in their personal situations and diverse motives thereby accepting their different learning trajectories.

A key idea here is recognising that different skills will provide different forms of returns to each student. One student may develop confidence in his or her ability to communicate using social media, thereby providing greater levels of control of that aspect of their life. Alternatively, another student may develop confidence in his or her ability to make sense of the environment, thereby accessing greater assurance in their ability to navigate their environs. Get the idea? In this regard, your curriculum should not be overly organised around subject-oriented learning. That is, our students are learning about themselves vis-à-vis an opportunity to solve a problem or create new value, not merely *about* the principles of entrepreneurship. As educators we need to draw our students into a non-rational world where their existing beliefs can be contradicted (Brookfield, 1990). This should preferably occur via collaborative learning processes that safely facilitate the student's *reintegration* into their community. By reintegration I mean that the student becomes reoriented towards aspects (previously not acknowledged) in their local environment that will ultimately relate to the consequences of their actions.

Clearly the above discussion affords an important role for student reflection, an issue that will be discussed more fully in chapter six. Prior to that discussion, I flag the importance of ensuring our students can engage in critical self-reflection. Are you interested in the life histories of each of your students? Do you invite each student to bring their life history into their learning environments? Can you appreciate the importance of allowing each student to locate their own *starting* point? Do you accept that the extent to which each student may reintegrate with their community will be based on their *prior* understanding of that community? If you are uncomfortable with these questions being posed, you may be demonstrating a tendency to remain the central figure of authority to you students. If you are already feeling your own emancipation you may be ready to assist your students in new and exciting ways.

In chapter ten various processes for enabling students to challenge their own existing assumptions (implicit or explicit) will be outlined. The key issue here is that all assumptions are challenged. The value of collaborative learning processes should be obvious. From my personal experience I am able to draw out inherent assumptions by using group discussions to surface cultural and socio-economic factors that may potentially distort a student's sense of their relationship to their surroundings. Likewise, the past life experience and the different levels of educational achievement also provide me with inputs that I can manipulate. As my students' dispositions, perceived status, motivations and values start to dominate the learning environment, something interesting invariably happens. A shared realisation emerges that they are all being challenged by the idea of creating something that doesn't yet exist.

Herein lies your challenge; moving students to an imaginary starting line. I say imaginary because it seems to be starting on the same day at roughly the same time. However, in reality each student holds a different life history that will impact differently upon their particular challenge. In chapter seven we will explore this issue via consideration of each student's resource profile. Until then, I challenge you to step back from the discussion presented within this chapter. Ask yourself are you an educator of course material or an architect of learning? Your answer to this question will help you to see why focusing on learning is so important. Without wanting to offend, most people can claim to be able to teach something, but only a few can demonstrate how their students learn as individuals.

Let us conclude where we started. Our lizards, despite their best intentions cannot connect purpose and consequence vis-à-vis planning the sex of their offspring. In many ways we suffer the same fate, with environmentally induced change a potential factor in all our activities. The major difference between ourselves and lizards being our advanced level of consciousness. As McKenzie (1934: 59) observed, 'the basic difference between human ecology and the ecologies of the lower organisms lies in the fact that man is capable of a higher level of behaviour in his adaptation process'. That is, we are able to discern more precisely the elements of the environment we interact with and most importantly, manipulate aspects of the environment to our advantage.

Having contemplated the process of change in our students and our potential role in this regard, attention must turn towards the *type* of student we might seek to create. In *Teaching Entrepreneurship to Undergraduates* the notion of the reasonable adventurer was advanced. However, there are several reasons why merely developing this type of graduate in a postgraduate context is not enough. This will be the focus of the next chapter.

PART II


The Nature of our Students

# 4.   The Tethered Adventurer

> Life consists in learning to live on one's own, spontaneous, freewheeling: to do this one must recognise what is one's own – be familiar and at home with oneself. This means basically learning who one is, and learning what one has to offer to the contemporary world, and then learning how to make that offering valid. The purpose of education is to show a person how to define himself authentically and spontaneously in relation to the world. (Merton, 1979: 3)

In this chapter I will offer for your consideration the idea of the *tethered adventurer* as the ideal type of postgraduate learner I would like to help create. It will first be useful to present my reasoning as to why the notion of the reasonable adventurer is incomplete within the postgraduate context. I say incomplete rather than inappropriate because the idea of the reasonable adventurer still has something to contribute to this discussion, but not enough to complete the conversation. The aim of this discussion is to get you to contemplate your ideal type of graduate. Contemplating such a student is important as it provides the starting point from which to work backwards from to construct the appropriate curriculum and learning environment.

Previously I have argued (Jones, 2011) that discovering Heath's (1964) idea of the reasonable adventurer enabled me to overcome the challenge of balancing undergraduate expectations against undergraduate capabilities. The use of the reasonable adventurer approach enables learning as an enterprising process to take centre stage. Students are relieved of the burden of having to assume they can conquer the world at age 20. In the place of such expectations, students can develop a confidence in their ability to create opportunities for satisfaction in the actual emerging reality that is their lives. By accident I was also able to retrospectively design a more accurate curriculum and learning environment having found a descriptor for my ideal graduate.

Having elevated the focus of our enquiry from undergraduate to postgraduate, I recognised problems in defaulting to the reasonable adventurer. As a graduate, the reasonable adventurer graduate bestows upon the student, six excellent attributes, those being; *intellectectuality, close friendships, independence in value judgements, a tolerance of ambiguity, a breadth of interest* and *a sense of humour.* However, these are attributes that enable graduates to essentially play a long game. Postgraduates quite often find themselves playing a very short game. That is, they need to match their developed self to an enterprising opportunity during the time of study, not several years after. What seemed to be missing was a more direct temporal connection between thinking, feeling and acting within the immediate moments of one's life. The reasonable adventurer is getting ready for what life has in store, but the tethered adventurer is embedded in the situations of their current life. In the case of the former, regarding the development of students, it has been noted that 'it is not what they are at eighteen, it is what they become afterwards that matters' Whitehead (1929: 1). With regards the latter, Skinner's (1964: 484) observation that 'education is what survives when what has been learnt has been forgotten' would seem more relevant.

To expand upon this point, as educators working with postgraduates, we don't have the luxury of not worrying about who our students are. We cannot simply leave it to fate as to who they might become, because as we encounter them, they are already situated in their lives. Thus, our concern should be on how they comprehend (or make sense of) their world. Given that education should have an aim, for me it is developing a student capable creating opportunities from the complexity of they're *situated* lives.

Having previously discovered the notion of self-authorship in the work of Marcia Baxter-Magolda (2004), I sensed an opportunity to reorganise of my thoughts. I offer you a glimpse into my thinking not to convince you to adopt my notion of the tethered adventurer, but rather to convince you of the validity of such thinking. Let us begin with an overview of the notion of self-authorship. Following this I will explain how in conjunction with the ideas related to the Heath's (1964) reasonable adventurer, the tethered adventurer emerged.

## CREATING THE TETHERED ADVENTURER

Originally developed by Kegan (1994), the notion of self-authoring has been developed significantly by the various works of Baxter-Magolda (2004; 2007; 2008). Defined succinctly as one's 'internal capacity to define one's beliefs, identity, and social relations' (Baxter-Magolda, 2008: 269), self-authorship is an established concept regarding how we can explain an individual's ability to cope with the challenges of adult life. In general terms I see the concept as a *grown up* version of the reasonable adventurer. In turn, I will argue shortly that I see the tethered adventurer as an individual who demonstrates the dimensions of self-authoring whilst also displaying a heighted sense of their surrounds and the nature of their interactions with all other entities.

Metaphorically speaking, we start the process of cocooning undergraduates when we attempt to develop the attributes of the reasonable adventurer. As noted elsewhere (Jones, 2011), we cannot always see our students emerge from this process as a beautiful butterfly because graduation tends to interrupt the process. However, as they leave behind the unwanted materials of their past life to emerge as a butterfly, I now see this as their first step towards self-authoring. Let me explain this process in more detail. The development of self-authorship involves helping our students to reshape 'what they believe (epistemology), their sense of self (intrapersonal), and their relationships with others (interpersonal)' (Meszaros, 2007: 11). The process of developing the reasonable adventurer attributes provides a wonderful precursor to what is ultimately required for self-authorship.

In terms of the epistemological dimension, students are challenged to view the world alternatively through the development of *intellectuality* and *close friendships*. They must demonstrate a capacity to alternate between being a believer and a sceptic. They are encouraged to discover the individuality of other students, to allow their view of the world to be challenged. Moving along to the intrapersonal dimension, the process of group sense making discussed in chapter six illustrates a simple process in which the manner of how the students view themselves is self-challenged. In addition, the importance of developing *value judgements* also contributes to students enfolding their emerging life experiences to reshape their understanding of themselves. Finally, the interpersonal dimension. The use of *humour* as a means of breaking down social relations provides some initial space for deeper friendships to form. These relationships are born from the challenges individuals collectively face in small groups where their *tolerance of ambiguity* is being developed task by task. The last factor that assists this process is the students need to find the solutions to their immediate problems through developing an uncommon interest in the commonplace, or extending their *breadth of interest*.

What is being claimed is that through offering my undergraduate students an opportunity to develop the six attributes of the reasonable adventure, I am perhaps positively shaping their capacity to also self-author as they gain greater command of their future lives. Of course, to state the obvious again, we can't guarantee that our students will take advantage of the self-development opportunities presented to them. As discussed in chapter two their motivations vary too much for them to move as a herd. Our challenge is to make the opportunities for self-development possible and achievable. That is, we must ensure the 'purpose of education is to show a person how to define himself [or herself] authentically and spontaneously in relation to the world' (Merton, 1979: 3). I think that in selling our students a notion of the type of graduate we aim to help create is a useful activity. Let us consider the views of some of my past students regarding their development as learners.

> I sense a new depth of understanding of where I get my energy from, how I prefer to gather information, how I prefer to make decisions and how I deal with outside forces (how I choose to behave around others). Also, learning how to manage myself when I am faced with or involved in a position where I cannot use my strengths. (student comment no. 1)

> I've always been a visual thinker and if I can't get my head around information I will pull it apart and put it into a table or a visual diagram until it works for me. I also liked the group work activities in class; they contribute to the social aspect of learning and establish relationships for pairing and sharing or study buddy situations, which I greet with open arms. The group sense making process helped me immensely. I am now able to follow a useful process when I can't make sense of a situation. I can now follow a sense-making path. (student comment no. 2)

> My learning style has evolved but stayed consistent to the style I identified during the course of my Graduate Certificate Business studies. I really benefited from actually discovering and understanding my style better and now know that it is alright to be the way I am and that others are actually like me! If anything, I can adapt to other learning styles more readily as an adult learner, relying upon the tacit knowledge derived from my tradesman/sportsman background. (student comment no. 3)

> While I have always taken the initiative to learn, previously I just wasn't brave enough to do something as radical as I have been doing in this class during the student presentations. However, this unit has made me braver. (student comment no. 4)

> I have learned to accept that my (Myers Briggs) ESTP personality type is ok. I always have held a thirst for knowledge, but my learning style seemed quite different from traditional methods. I now know its ok! The tacit and codified knowledge in my head is extremely valuable. I will continue to study in some shape or form. It excites me. (student comment no. 5)

Across this selection of comments is a sense of self-discovery. The gains made by the students is less about the content and more about their own personal development. Given the centrality of the individual in the process of entrepreneurship (Aldrich and Martinez, 2001), it is critical our students understand themselves as learners and actors in the process of entrepreneurship. My biases in this regard are discussed here and elsewhere (Jones, 2011), and should not be interpreted as an argument for what is the best type of graduate we should aim to be developing. If we consider the nature of opinion from around the globe, it is clear there is much more opportunity for future debate.

## WHAT TYPE OF GRADUATE TO CREATE?

Respondents to the IE-II survey nominated several quite closely related types of graduates they associated with postgraduate EE. Figure 2.1 illustrates these types; ranging from simply developing better managers or students with better knowledge of business, to more entrepreneurial graduates who might also actually start-up. The most common type of graduate was a student who was simply more entrepreneurial. Or as Kelly Smith of the University of Huddersfield in England noted, one that is enterprising – able to spot opportunities and make them happen in their work/research/life. Or, as suggested by Professor Lars Kolvereid from the University of Nordland in Sweden, a graduate who is innovative, creative, action oriented, and opportunity seeking.

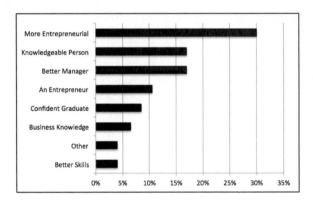

*Figure 4.1   Nominated graduate types*

Clearly, the context the respondents contribute from matters. For example, Associate Professor Alex Maritz at the Swinburne University of Technology in Australia saw the development of bona fide entrepreneurs from his Masters of Entrepreneurship and Innovation course, whereas he saw the need to only develop entrepreneurial intentionality in his other Masters courses. In terms of creating the entrepreneur, Janice Gates at the Western Illinois University in America argued for the development of a graduate who has the skills necessary to plan, start, and keep a small venture going. Alternatively, in terms of the intentionality, the diversity within student cohorts could clearly influence such aims. Annette Naudin at Birmingham City University in England did not nominate any specific type of graduate. Her reasoning being that they have high levels of international students. As a result, it is too broad a category to define. Thus she sees the need to default a proactive approach, developing enterprising students, not necessarily for start-up. Perhaps sitting between these perspectives was the response of Peter Balan at the University of South Australia in Australia who leaned towards a person who is more open to being an enterprising person, and someone who is more ready to work with an entrepreneur to establish a new venture.

From my personal perspective, it was pleasing to see support for a *knowledgable graduate* emerge amongst many of the responses. Professor David Rae at Lincoln University in England asked is there just one type? He then queried, how about adaptive knowledgeable person? Building on such questions, **Dr Jane Nolan at the University of Cambridge in England** argued for the need to create critical, reflective learners who can go on learning throughout their lives and who have high levels of self efficacy to sustain them. Or as Dr Susan Rushworth at the Swinburne University of Technology in Australia articulates, a graduate who is a self-directed adult capable of creating change in the way they choose. Such opinions provide further confidence in my own thinking in this respect.

The last type of graduate cleanly articulated was that of the confident graduate. Dr Bill Kirkley at Massey University in New Zealand saw the value in creating graduates who have a strong sense of their independence, are ambitious and have the confidence in their ability to generate creative and innovative solutions to new opportunities. Likewise, Dr Briga Hynes at the Kemmy Business School in Ireland sought to develop well-rounded, creative and confident graduates who are able to contribute to the social and economic landscape they operate in.

In summary, in amongst so many different and closely related notions of what postgraduate EE should be producing, I see a place for the tethered adventurer. Importantly, as previously noted, because I can visualize the place of the tethered adventurer in my aims and the role I play in creating such a graduate I am capable of contemplating the nature of the curriculum required to challenge my students. This chapter will conclude by offering you an opportunity to reflect more deeply upon the nature of your thinking in this regard. In essence, to what extent do you feel confident there is alignment between your curriculum and the nature of the graduate/s you seek to create.

# DEVELOPING YOUR IDEAL GRADUATE

I truly believe the EE has been held back from getting closer to its potential contribution to society through its close relationship to the business school. Business schools tend to focus almost exclusively of content derived from textbooks and other bodies of assumed known facts. This would be fine if our ideal graduate was a walking and talking encyclopedia. But, I am yet to meet an entrepreneur in need of such a disposition. From this perspective, the *outcome* relates to a body of knowledge and the ability to educators to communicate it, students to absorb it (at least temporarily) and for a process of assessment to evaluate the students success or otherwise in knowing such content. I would argue strongly that this is of little use for EE.

EE is about transformations, developing graduates capable of creating that which doesn't yet exist, using ideas born from imaginative recombination and/or raw speculation. More importantly, for postgraduate students of EE, they are in 'grave danger of growing' (Kegan, 1994: 293) as their practical goals collide with their newfound curiosity of life and it's opportunities. They have little need to become repositories of someone else's favorite pieces of information. They have the right to seek information relevant to such goals and to seek to transcend such information (Hart, 2001) in ways that embodies a mastery of their life's pursuits. There is a need for our postgraduate students to better understand the meaning of their experiences, to become expert witnesses to their unfolding adventures and to engage in critical reflections of their actions and subsequent outcomes (see Taylor, 2000).

To what extent are we in agreement? To what extent are we in agreement but you feel prevented from acting in ways that might satisfy your students' developmental needs? To what extent are you a practitioner of self-development? My related ideas of the reasonable and tethered adventurers represent only my current thinking. They need not be evaluated as ideals or benchmarks. They serve only as a window into my mind and as potential stimulus to your own thinking. Who is your ideal graduate? Is there a baseline type from which other variants can emerge? Or, are your thoughts in this area held hostage by institutional forces that assume your graduate must be a walking and talking encyclopedia, at least while their batteries hold their charge.

A great place to start this journey in terms of either actually starting it, or verifying you're most recent past steps, is to engage with the literature of student development. As educators we are blessed to be able to access such a broad range of perspectives in this area. The challenge remains finding a niche that suits your approach and is applicable to your students' learning contexts. Like our teaching philosophies, we typically already hold a view of our perfect graduate; we perhaps have never been required to articulate the nature of such a student. The real power that flows from such articulation is the clarity that is delivered to you in terms of being able to look backwards from the assumed development of such students. Holding a picture in your mind of those students, and their various learning pathways, ensures you can now start to envisage the curriculum and matching learning environment required to make them a reality.

In terms of the various learning pathways your students have encountered and will ultimately encounter, you hold very little influence in this area. We are not working with fresh-faced undergraduates waiting for their moment in the sun. Our postgraduates come to us with the scars of their actual life experiences. This ultimately is the gift bestowed upon us as educators, another challenge for us to convert in our quest to be excellent educators. This challenge forms to focus of the following chapter.

# 5. Exploiting Student Experience

> Learning with and from each other is a necessary and important aspect of all courses. The role it plays varies widely and the forms it takes are very diverse, but without it students gain an impoverished education. (Boud, 2001: 2)

In 2006 I had the privilege to spend several days wandering around Harvard Business School (HBS). A colleague, who up until that point in time had been employed at HBS had invited me to observe the inner workings of their case study method. While there were many aspects of the method to be impressed by, the thing that stood out the most was the extent to which the students learnt from each other. This chapter makes an important contribution to the overall argument being made regarding our students' development.

My visit to HBS started with a quick tour of the school and its lovely surroundings. Then, I retired to my hotel room to swat up on the first case study I would observe. My mind was literally bamboozled by the breadth and complexity of the HBS case I was trying to digest. I eventually fell asleep, saved by my jetlag from a mountain of data and detail that seemed beyond my comprehension. I awoke with excitement, the opportunity of seeing first-hand a method that was lauded by some and criticised by others. As I sat at the back of the classroom, my colleague skilfully led the conversation in subtle ways, drawing in opinion from expected corners and, ensuring the process towards eventual decision-making, stayed on track. Ninety minutes later as the students filed out and the blackboards were being washed down, I was amazed at the diversity of opinion shared, of the insightfulness of the arguments made and of the clarity of decision-making presented. I thought to myself, surely these men and woman must be the best of the best.

I felt truly humbled to be in the presence of what could easily be the future leaders of the United States business landscape. How did they attract such talented graduates back into education? How could these students possibly know so much about so many aspects of business? How was my colleague able to orchestrate such a seamless conversation that culminated in such a clean outcome? How could these students now simply move on from the complexity of this case and onto the next case I would witness the following day, a case that seemed even more complicated? Thankfully, the answers to these questions emerged over the course of the next few days. Of most interest was the answer I found to the issue of how the students became so knowledgable about so many separate aspects of business.

As I strolled through Spangler Hall, the primary residence of the students, an active business hub for their various entrepreneurial talents, I stumbled onto the student lounges. There, I met many friendly students who took the time to accommodate my curiosity. In reality it took but a few questions and just a little observation to inform myself of one of the HBS secrets. The students were not selected for their potential genius. Sure, they had demonstrated excellent progress in their respective careers and had demonstrated sound undergraduate results. However, it was clear that the high degree of knowledge I had observed during the case study process was greatly influenced by their ability to work with one another.

HBS is a unique place; it affords excellent students the opportunity to become aware of, and influenced by, the career specific knowledge already developed by fellow students. Experts in logistics rubbed elbows in the student lounge with experts in accounting, economics, marketing, information systems, operations management and all manner of specialisation; and vice versa. Their individual preparation for the cases was turbo-charged through positive interaction within which mutual gains were continuously shared. It was as if HBS had waited for each student to develop sufficient expertise in their chosen area of specialisation before assembling them all together. If only we could be so lucky to have at our disposal such knowledgable and talented students.

## THE SOCIAL FACTOR

In reality, we may never be so lucky. However, this need not matter. What is of most importance is that we comprehend the value of social interaction and knowledge sharing as highlighted above. It would seem obvious that our students stand to gain much from each other, even if they are starting from a lower base of perceived sophistication than students at HBS. I say perceived, because in reality many of our students have gained more work and life experience than students at HBS. The really big issue relates to whether or not we recognise this and if we are capitalising upon it.

Let me tell you another story from a recent class that highlights the unique contributions our students can potentially make. Twice a year I work with students in a class where I introduce them to a sense-making framework (to be discussed in chapter 8) and also to the opportunities that can occur from developing confidence with social media. This class always starts with the students introducing themselves and providing a short background of their adult life and their hopes for participation in the class. Recently, a student in this class introduced himself in a very humble way. I suspect he felt in awe of the local Mayor and other more publicly know individuals. He told us he was a builder by trade, and that of recent times he had been playing around with social media *fan* pages. None of us really knew what this meant, and instead of delving a little deeper into his new-found interests, we moved onto the next student. At that very moment we missed an opportunity to be educated about the true nature of opportunities in the world of social media.

A few weeks later when the students had returned to class, the student who had been playing around with fan pages stood up to present to the class. The nature of this presentation was relatively straightforward. They would discuss their chosen idea and it's importance to their local region. They would demonstrate their understanding of the sense-making framework and inform the class how their thinking around their idea had changed via their use of the framework. They would conclude with a list of challenges that remain vis-à-vis their possible exploitation of the idea. What followed next was one of the unforgettable moments in anyone's teaching careers.

The student then proceeded to inform us of the magnitude of his escapades. He had been drawn into to the world of fan pages and had developed a very successful fan page for an emerging talent who had become genuinely famous through his appearance on a reality talent show in the UK. His new-found skills and direct interaction with the emerging star had led to invitations to fly to the UK and meet the rest of the developing entourage. A builder by trade, his natural skills and genuine interest in the emerging star's development had been well and truly noticed and rewarded.

At present, the now ex-builder is increasingly involved in managing a broader set of activities for the emerging star and is fielding offers to manage other new aspiring talents from other parts of the globe. He has become the authoritative figure to his fellow students regarding all things social media. I ask him for guidance and he gladly assists, as his incredibly humble disposition. While this example has elements that are unlikely to be the norm, it nevertheless demonstrates the latent potential of our students to assist in their collective development, regardless of how unaspiring they may seem on first glance.

The obvious question it would seem, what is standing in the way of us continuously searching for any such intelligence to share within our cohorts? We know our students are a diverse bunch of individuals. We know they have developed intelligence in a range of different and potentially complementary areas. I suspect a major obstacle is the role we are expected to play in the classroom, be it as educator or more broadly as facilitator.

## THE STRENGTH OF VULNERABILITY

I have previously argued (Jones, 2011: 13) with reference to the work of Parker Palmer 'that good teaching matters less about methods and more about the degree to which we as educators know and trust ourselves. That there is a need to be vulnerable to the students and the learning environments we operate within'. That we should assist our students to learn about a truly complex subject through the infusion of imagination and reflection as encouraged by us the educators. I believe strongly that we are the custodians of little more that our students collective experiences. It is we who introduce them and it is we who frame the rules of how deep these introductions should be across the each entire cohort. Our willingness to be vulnerable to their potential contributions is key. It is a good thing that they may inject something into the learning of others that goes beyond our personal contribution.

This I hold is the mark of a good educator, the willingness not to frame the limitations of our students' learning in parallel to our own cognitive bases. When we communicate to our postgraduate students that we are looking forward to meeting them and having an opportunity to learn from them we send a powerful invitation. We are saying to them, don't attend class as a passive student; come along as an active student with something to share. It has been recognised that the best teachers (see Bain, 2004: 72) 'tended to look for and appreciate the individual value of each student'. Are you doing this? Are you explicitly informing your students that you need their help? That we can achieve much from tackling this subject area with all hands on deck, rather than a heroic leader stationed on the quarterdeck. It is interesting to see what insights emerge from the IE-II survey in this respect.

## GLOBAL PERSPECTIVES

Respondents were asked how might we as educators harness the experience of our postgraduate students to increase the learning opportunities of all students. The simplest approach stated by Professor Don B Bradley III of the University of Central Arkansas in the United States who felt it important to have his students share their experiences. Likewise, Dr Loykie Lomine at the University of Winchester in England felt important to give students the chance, through activities, to use and share their knowledge. Indeed, Katie Wray at Newcastle University in the United Kingdom saw the novel opportunity to develop peer-mentoring modules, postgraduates teaching undergraduates and gain credit from their development and reflection. Such an activity would clearly elevate the knowledge bases of the postgraduate student. Janice Gates at the Western Illinois University in America supported this sentiment, noting that she had a mixed class of postgraduates and undergraduates and that the postgraduates were always willing to share what they have experienced. In addition, she also used the postgraduates as a source for contacts for potential guest speakers. Similar ideas were expressed by Dr Jane Nolan at the University of Cambridge in England, who argued for the development of supportive communities in which such experience can be shared and reflected upon.

The thoughts of Dr Susan Rushworth at the Swinburne University of Technology in Australia extend these ideas. Susan also supported the use of guest speakers, using Postgraduate students as mentors for undergraduate students and generally sharing experiences with their classmates. She felt such processes could produce intense, personal, and therefore powerful, learning experiences, once trust is created. Dr Bill Kirkley at Massey University in New Zealand agreed that by harnessing such experience and releasing it back into the learning environment through debate, challenging exercises, and reflective practice, significant learning was achievable. As I contemplate these last two contributions, a concern is emerging in my mind around the idea of vulnerability. Susan raises the issue of trust and Bill identifies the personal nature of surfacing such experience and then releasing it back into the learning environment. The following contributors identify a factor that I sense is central to such discussion, that of failure.

Dr Alicia Castillo, an entrepreneur and invited lecturer at the University of Western Australia feels that if we can first help students recognise that we are all different and right in some way, diversity then becomes a blessing. She also thought we need to help students think about failure as a possibility; this is more relevant in Australia and Europe than in other countries. Alicia has used Carol Dweck's (2006) book *Mindset* to help put learning (not success or failure) in the context of continuous improvement. From a similar perspective, Tony Watts for the Metropolitan Small Business Centre in Australia felt we don't just need to harness people's life experience, we need to build on it and get them to reflect on what worked and what didn't. The hardest part of the process he argued was introducing them to the concept of productive failure. Like Alicia, he felt Australians are not culturally attuned to value failure.

I know this to be an important issue. As educators facilitating a challenging and hopefully productive and transformational experience we need to ensure students feel safe. Clearly, there is no switch that can be simply flicked to convert our students' thinking in this regard. We need to win their confidence and allow them to experience the nature of the environment for themselves. Peter Balan of the University of South Australia in Australia uses workshop exercises to replace a lot of his lecturing. This means that his postgraduate students spend most of their class time discussing real-life challenges related to starting up a new technology, or social venture. This gives plenty of opportunity for postgraduate students to test their ideas and experiences against those of others. Importantly, I suspect it also creates a social process within which respect, appreciation and friendship can also develop. Annette Naudin at Birmingham City University in England also hinted at the need for pro-active planning by the educator, suggesting that we should allow more time for discussion and presentations from the students. Essentially advocating that the traditional role of the teacher be transformed into that of a facilitator.

Finally, Monica Kreuger, President of Global Infobrokers in Canada, sums up many other views calling for more facilitation in workshops where the students must develop their own scenarios and answers, presenting these back to the larger group; self reflection and assessment approaches and tools that require students to integrate life experience; connect students from different parts of the world where shared experience is now opening their eyes to global possibilities; identifying and approaching entrepreneurs they know in the community as live case studies; and identifying opportunities from their life experience. Across all the contributions there is a common theme. The educator's role is being challenged. In order to achieve greater involvement from our students it would seem that we must alter the traditional role they may expect us to perform. For me this entails using the inherent diversity of my students to our collective benefit.

## SURFACING THE DIVERSITY

I have demonstrated elsewhere (see Jones, 2011) that as educators in our field we will most certainly face high levels of student diversity. In the context of postgraduate education my suspicions are not merely confirmed, but extended. The question remains, how to use such diversity productively? Further, how to use such diversity in ways that will assist you to build trust within your cohort and take the edge off any fears they hold? Many of the respondents to the survey on this issue noted the importance of reflection. I concur, this is an important process through which students can internalize not only their own learning but also the feelings and challenges of other students.

My experiences tell me that using diversity to advance the opportunities for student learning can be a very powerful tool. The process I use is called group sense-making. I use this process to disarm my students, to draw them into a web of trust and deep introspection. Rather than asking them to reflect on an issue as it relates to or impacts them, I require them to engage in a process of meta-reflection.

The aim of the group sense-making process is to expose my students to the differences and similarities that exist between them. Essentially, I am aiming to use these differences and similarities to aid their learning. The process is designed to cultivate a deeper appreciation of each student's personal feelings, whilst simultaneously enabling students to appreciate the feelings of the other students in the class. The process is completed through four phases, which are proceeded by a situation statement. The aim of the situation statement is to provide the educator with a provocative instrument around which to focus attention. The four phases are as follows:

**Phase 1**

Students are asked to identify and record the personal feelings they experience upon reading the situation statement. It is quite likely they may experience more than one feeling. Conflicting feelings and/or those feelings that change over time should be noted. It is important that they don't only note the assumed or described feelings, but also their actual feelings.

**Phase 2**

Having viewed the responses of other classmates, each student now attempts to make sense of the situation statement, using the perspectives of all involved group members. They use the feelings reported to develop a sense of meaning vis-à-vis the collective feelings reported by their classmates. This analysis may incorporate an exploration of personal beliefs, dispositions, experiences and attitudes. They conclude by stating explicitly what they believe it all to mean.

**Phase 3**

Each individual student now attempts to validate their own analysis of the situation by asking for input from someone not involved in the first two phases. In other words, the meaning attributed to the situation is confirmed (or disconfirmed) with reference to the ideas and perspectives of others and/or through personal reflection of their own personal experiences.

**Phase 4**

Each student indicates how reflection on the situation has influenced their approach and/or perspective to this specific issue. Any possible shift in values, beliefs, attitudes and/or general awareness is also noted. The following comments are illustrative of a student's progress through the four phases. In this particular actual example, the situation statement (see Appendix 2) focuses upon my perceptions of different types of entrepreneurs I see in society, and the possibility of a honourable defeat.

## Phase 1

The situation statement made me FEEL inspired by the notion that entrepreneurship is not solely the domain of the most gifted, the most talented or the brightest. Instead a view that we are all capable of entrepreneurship pervades and replaces the heroic view held by many of the rugged-individualist, self-starter entrepreneur.

However it made me FEEL frustrated by the notion that our classroom's individual diversity can be defined by labels, such as worker, servant, saviour or creator. These prejudices are a reflection of societal biases, often based on over simplification and ignorance, which have no place in a university classroom that seeks to grow knowledge and capacity in its students.

Finally, I FEEL indifferent to those who choose a honourable retreat, for it is an individual's prerogative, whether they choose to apply the learning's in their lives. However, having completed the unit one would trust that this cohort will have a broader appreciation of what entrepreneurship is, in the hope that it breaks down the over simplified notion that entrepreneurship is a one size fits all approach that infests society. (Student A's phase 1 comment)

## Phase 2

After reading the other students feelings towards the situation statement it is clear that within a small cohort there has been a diverse and mixed reaction. Perhaps this is consistent with broader society's views on entrepreneurship, formed by generational biases and the championing of individual success, primarily measured in monetary terms, covered in detail by the media in contemporary society.

There were different views on whether entrepreneurship is a pathway trodden by a few gifted opportunists or whether this label of success permeates a wider group in society. I was interested in Student Z's view that he felt the heroic definition of entrepreneurship was self-limiting and I draw from this that some may be intimidated by the prevailing definition of entrepreneurship. I resonate with Student Y's view that entrepreneurship is not necessarily about 'making a squillion dollars' and supports my view that entrepreneurship is not a one size fits all concept.

There were also differences on how the students felt towards an honorable exit. Some suggest this is an easy way out, or an excuse for those who float through life bereft of ambition or drive. This differs from my view and some other students who accept that we cannot all be entrepreneurs. It also raises the issue of social and economic disadvantage and whether we all have the same opportunities. However some may argue that opportunities are made regardless of an individual's socio-economic influences. Several students discussed their uneasiness of labelling individuals into groups, suggesting that this is rigid and limiting. This was consistent with my views. However a couple of students indicated acceptance of this practice.

When I look at the other student's postings, I THINK THIS MEANS that there are divergent views on entrepreneurship amongst this cohort, which are consistent with broader society's views. This is not unexpected as a concept as broad as entrepreneurship is likely to generate different emotions and is likely to be skewed by pre-conditioning and society's contemporary influences. To some it's about individual success and monetary gain, while for others it may be about a social cause and a desire to effect change. I think that entrepreneurship is present in many areas of society, in private and public enterprise, is driven by individuals or groups, and whose purpose and goals is as varied as the loose label of entrepreneurship. (Student A's phase 2 comment)

## Phase 3

I asked my wife to read the situation statement and give me her views on what she thought it meant. She believed that the statement meant entrepreneurship was not a select club, rather it was open to those who are prepared to work hard, apply themselves in pursuit of a goal. She didn't conform to the view that entrepreneurship is for a select group, rather it is based on merit and achievement. She said that an individual can create their own pathways, which are several and numerous if he/she remains flexible and is not fixated on one path. She felt that personality type is a critical determinant of which pathway an individual will choose, suggesting that some individuals are risk takers while others are conservative and these types will affect the outcome. She was accepting of diversity and felt the labels were unimportant.

Her comments VALIDATED my feelings and views on the situation statement. In summary we both agree that a narrow definition of a rugged-individualist, self-starter entrepreneur doesn't encapsulate the broader aspects of the subject. Furthermore, she VALIDATED my view that labels are unimportant and that an individual's pathway is their prerogative. However her view that entrepreneurship is solely up to an individual differs from mine in so far as I still believe social and economic opportunity will influence the success or otherwise of an individual's pursuit of entrepreneurship. Her discussion on personality type indicators was interesting as I had not considered this aspect, so this broadened my opinions. (Student A's phase 3 comment)

## Phase 4

This process has been interesting and has VALIDATED my initial views, which are undoubtedly shaped by my values. However, I have been accepting of other people's ideas and this has added to my reflections and appreciation on the subject. The divergent opinions has VALIDATED my view that entrepreneurship is a broad subject, unable to be easily labeled and one that is over simplified in society and regrettably primarily measured largely by monetary gain, which perpetuates the limiting definition of a rugged-individualist, self-starter entrepreneur. Upon reflection I think it is important that as one advances through the process, not to seek like-minded students whose feelings and opinions align with mine, as the real value is in exploring alternative views to better understand the subject matter. (Student A's phase 4 comment)

What is evident from the above comments by student A is his recognition as to how access to a process that taps into student diversity has benefited him. As I have stated previously (Jones, 2011), it is of great benefit to me as an educator to have a ringside seat throughout this process as well. Rather than merely allowing the student to reflect, the provision of group sense making allows multiple perspectives to be shared by students and the educator. I can use this process proactively to increase individual student learning outcomes through the development of well-crafted situation statements. I believe this process to be central to the genuine possibility of student transformation. My never-ending challenge being to ensure that the students can see how engagement with this diversity is beneficial to their learning.

## STEPPING UP TO THE ROLE OF FACILITATOR

In summary, this chapter presents you with a challenge, one that tests your commitment to being the best educator you can be. As educators we all have fears and so do our students. When we ask them to step into our shoes as facilitators of learning, then we most likely expose such fears. What steps do you need to take to gain the trust of your students? What steps do you need to take to enable them to trust each other? What strategies are used elsewhere to engender trust and a supportive environment where concerns about perceived failure and embarrassment are addressed?

Perhaps some of the answers you seek may be found in the following chapter. I believe that adapting to the role of facilitator of learning within diverse cohorts of students requires much lateral thinking. Further, that our perceptions of how students experience education always requires careful consideration. If you have made it this far into the book then I suspect you already have what it takes to successfully deliberate on such matters. Let us now turn our attention to the notion of the extended learning environment.

# 6.　The Extended Learning Environment

We live in a world were the very nature of the classroom is being questioned. If we are not flipping them (Bergmann and Sams, 2012) or using technology to stay one step ahead of the MOOC threat, we are scheduling our interaction with students at times that may seem unconventional. Regardless of how we approach such matters the fact remains we are responsible for creating the conditions that will best assist our students. Be that the setup of the physical classroom, the availability of materials online, the timing of interaction to facilitate thinking and also exploration space. What was once taken for granted now requires much deliberation.

This chapter is not lengthy, but its importance cannot be overlooked. Our ability to create meaningful interaction through which trust is developed is impacted significantly by our efforts in this area. For example, some of the most meaningful interaction I have observed has occurred at the local hotel over a drink. One of my postgraduate classes occurs a good four hours drive from my home. When I visit this region, I stay two nights and let my past students know I am in town. In doing so, I invite them to catch up for a drink. This serves two distinct, yet related purposes. First, I am able to stay in touch with past students and hopefully gain insights into their adventures and to see what specifically from our initial time together has benefited them most. Second, I extend this invitation to my new students and enjoy introducing them to past students. Their conversations tend to make my life easier as the ambiguity associated with their forthcoming challenges become clear in the wisdom of hindsight. While the official instructions that connect my institution, my students and myself do not mention this activity, perhaps they should, such is the value of the process.

Put simply, we cannot assume that what matters to our students will occur under our control or even be observed by us. As we introduce a greater focus upon reflective exercises we increase the likelihood that their aha moments will happen in a time and place devoid of our presence. But this is the way it should be because when the situated learner synchronizes with life it will be at a time and place of their choosing. What we can do however is be increasingly mindful of what *thinking* processes are required to complete the challenges we set and seek to ensure we support such thinking. We also need to recognise that our students start from different points in their individual development.

There are numerous adult development theories that one can acquaint themselves with (Drago-Severson, 2009: 33). One in particular, constructive-development theory 'focuses on a person as an active meaning maker of experience, considering cognitive, affective, interpersonal, and intrapersonal experiences'. In particular it incorporates an important role for self-authoring, a component of my notion of the tethered adventurer. In a sense the learning environment must be supportive of providing each student with their own set of *adaptive challenges*. In order to succeed in this environment the student 'requires new approaches and, often, increased developmental capacities' to work through their challenges (Drago-Severson, 2009: 275).

The constructive-development framework of Kegan (1982) enables us as educators to work with students as individuals. It allows both parties to be cognisant of how they are identified as a learner and how they can know of objects. The key issue being that the learning environment must provide sufficient physical and mental space to allow for self-transformation. Elsewhere (see Jones, 2011) I have alluded to the value of the work of Beard and Wilson (2002). In the context of this discussion, I believe their ideas offer much potential value. It is one thing to acknowledge the possible different ways of knowing associated with the constructive-development framework; it is another to design a learning environment that can accommodate the self-develop of our individual students.

In previous chapters we have considered issues of motivation, diversity, the importance of experiential learning and the embedded situation of our learners. When we think about their learning environment I argue it is more about *their* learning environment and less about *our* teaching environment. So much of the progress they need to make will come from what drives them internally and influences their ability to interact with the social world. Just as entrepreneurship can be a very lonely journey so can such self-development. Let us consider more closely the ideas of Beard and Wilson (2002).

## THREE DIMENSIONS OF INFLUENCE

At the heart of Beard and Wilson's (2002) work is a desire to comprehend how we as educators can stimulate the senses of our students; to ensure they engage in deeper thinking and learning. They have developed a unique focus on the outer world of the learner, the sensory interface of the learner and the inner world of the learner. In the outer world of the learner, as educators, we are invited to consider the *places* where specific learning *activities* occur. So we are concerned with accommodating novel factors that may impact the learning process. For example, seeking validation of one's ideas from key stakeholders places the nascent entrepreneur within harms way. Consider the place of rejection and frustration in the place of our students' enquiry. Consider the challenge of freeing ones self from the constraints typical of daily life in order to find the time to pursue an idea. Consider being in the presence of a perceived experienced entrepreneur and feeling inadequate. These are just a few examples of the elements of the extended learning environment our students encounter. Such elements are typically not spoken of in pedagogical terms; but they exist in the place of our students' learning. At some point we may need to accept that we may assert little control over our students' place of learning.

One of our greatest challenges as educators is to create meaningful activities from which to challenge and engage our learners. To be able to develop challenges that are general enough to be spread across an entire cohort, yet specific enough to test any individual student. To also ensure the nature of the challenge developed provides a relatively equal starting point for each student; a tough ask when we factor in the natural diversity we are confronted with. In essence, we need to work towards designing activities that ensure the advent of experience; for experience is what lies at the heart of our students' movement towards self-development. Clearly, part of our challenge is to offer a variety of activities from within which pre-existing skills can be used and desirable skills developed vis-à-vis each individual student. Having contemplated the *where* and *what* of the learning environment, it is now time to consider *how* our students will experience such an environment.

Let us now consider the sensory interface of the learner. What senses will your students rely upon to navigate this extended learning environment you loosely facilitate? Will they rely upon their ability to speak? Will they rely upon their ears and/or their eyes? Will they rely upon their nerves and/or their gut intuition? Can we design tasks that require multiple senses to be used collectively? Beard and Wilson (2002) argue that when students use more senses in a particular activity it potentially increases the memorability of the learning experience due to more neural connections being used. Clearly, our ability to design *what* our students do can also include consideration of *how* they will do it as well.

Next, the inner world of the learner, here we must aim to ensure our students' *hearts* are in their efforts. We must aim to eliminate boredom and fear from their approach. We must aim to excite and provide hope in their ability to tackle and complete the tasks we design. I truly believe that this factor is of critical importance. My experiences with the group sense making process have afforded me a window into the hearts of my students. I have been able to observe the different feelings my students hold towards the various tasks they experience. Critically, such observations also allow me to contemplate how I will alter or retain aspects of my learning tasks.

Developing such an intimate understanding of my students' feelings also brings me closer towards seeing their *thinking*. It also enables me to see the diversity of thinking present in my students and to find ways for them to demonstrate to each other the various forms of intelligence. Again, as the facilitator we have an opportunity to contemplate the types of thinking we feel our students we benefit from developing.

Lastly, we need to ask how our learners can be encouraged to *change*. In chapter 3 we discussed the nature of the degree of difficulty, motivational state and feedback required to take advantage of brain plasticity in adults. Regardless of your particular approach, if you and your students view learning as a process of change, then engaging experiences combined with appropriate reflection will undoubtedly lead to a desire to change. This is a complex issue, and I have not done justice to the work of Beard and Wilson (2002), beyond introducing the essence of their ideas. Hopefully your interest in these matters has been sufficiently aroused. When I contemplate the responses to the IE-II survey I suspect this is an issue for us all.

## GLOBAL PERSPECTIVES

I sense many challenges for educators emerging on the horizon. The increasing usage of online technologies, of quality control processes and forms of blended learning. These issues all remove and/or restrict some of our control over how we manage the learning environments our students' engage/create. Dr Alicia Castillo from the Wealthing Group in Australia senses that we are already over lecturing ... she doesn't lecture, she assumes students come prepared and she doesn't encourage mere participation but *smart* participation. Alicia always wraps up classes with what they learned. This is an issue I frequently encounter in conversations with other educators. How to ensure our students can perform the role we desire them to perform?

Kelly Smith of the University of Huddersfield in England observes that often those who do not want to engage won't attend. Kelly has put an additional session into induction to set the scene as to what is expected of them, but subsequent sessions are optional and non-attendance remains a risk. Likewise, Assistant Professor Eric Liguori at California State University in America also notes that those students who do not attend class typically remain unengaged. For Dr Susan Rushworth at the Royal Melbourne Institute of Technology in Australia, any such absence matters. Susan noted that in terms of the delivered content, classroom attendance doesn't matter. In terms of making the theory *real*, it's extremely valuable. Not so much for hearing the lecturer, but for learning from each other. Despite social media and web-based learning environments, it's much harder to do this online.

An additional challenge for us here relates to the nature of challenges we design for our students. Drago-Severson (2009: 274-275) identifies technical and adaptive challenges. 'Technical problems are those for which we both understand the problem and can identify solutions to it, even if we need to call upon others for help'. Alternatively, adaptive challenges 'involve situations in which neither the problem nor the solution is completely known'. I suspect we are the latter. For example, Dr Denise Baden at the University of Southampton in England does not restrict her students to the classroom, Denise gets them devising ideas, doing market research, feasibility studies and field work helping social enterprises to expose them to alternative value systems. Likewise, Dr Elena Rodriguez-Falcon at Sheffield University in England states that her approach is very much dependent on particular students. For those who choose to engage on extracurricular activities, their learning is enhanced dramatically.

## SUMMARY

The learning environment and its many elements remains a largely unexplored area of pedagogy and andragogy. Given our propensity to use high levels of experiential learning, to aim to transform our learners and to create confidence in our graduates, we have little choice but to explore some more. The brief introduction to the work of Beard and Wilson (2002) should hopefully motivate you to reflect upon the elements of the learning environments you facilitate. Hopefully you can also accept that there is a significant amount of these environments that you cannot create or control. This is where most of our challenges lie. As argued in chapter 3, we need to contemplate the mechanisms through which our students may change and design our learning environments to accommodate such processes.

# 7.    The Resource Profile

There are things we know that we know. There are known unknowns. That is to say there are things that we now know we don't know. But there are also unknown unknowns. There are things we do not know we don't know. So when we do the best we can and we pull all this information together, and we then say well that's basically what we see as the situation, that is really only the known knowns and the known unknowns. And each year, we discover a few more of those unknown unknowns. (Donald Rumsfeld, 2002)

While a great deal of mirth has been generated by the above quote, in reality it hints at the reality that is ever-present in the lives of our students. In *Teaching Entrepreneurship to Undergraduates* I expressed trepidation about the typical resource profile of my 20 something year old undergraduate students. I am not too sure that my concerns have improved greatly within the domain of postgraduate education. First, lets recap on the basics of what is a resource profile.

## THE RESOURCE PROFILE

The success or failure of an entrepreneurial endeavour will most likely be explainable with direct reference to resource profile that an individual or group will hold relative to that opportunity (Aldrich and Martinez, 2001). A resource profile comprises human, financial and social capital. It is argued that what we know and who we know, combined with our ability to gain access and control of vital resources, go a long way to explaining our potential entrepreneurial success. Previously (Jones, 2011), I have proposed a basic fatal flaw in this seemingly obvious logic vis-à-vis its use in EE. Our undergraduates' reality is the same as everyone else's. The opportunities our students pursue are not shielded from the realities of the world. Accepting this proposition requires of EE educators a capacity to be candid about when and how EE students should engage with entrepreneurial opportunities. My concerns about resource profile development (or the lack of it) are illustrated in Figure 6.1 below. I typically see my undergraduates placed to far away from their visions in terms of the social, human and financial capital required to bring their visions to reality.

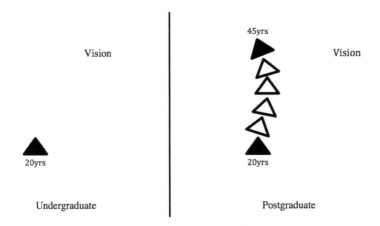

*Figure 7.1   Comparing resource profiles*

As noted elsewhere (Jones, 2011), I use a series of strategies to address the nature of this gap. I ask the students to consider the nature of the gap and to contemplate what would be required to close it, thereby *upsizing* their resource profile. I also invite the students to attempt a task within which their resource profile limitations will be highlighted by the reality of the actual outcomes. This process of *downsizing* enables the reality of any future gap to be seen through first-hand experience. Finally, I ask the students to contemplate what it might be like to *fit* their existing resource profile to an idea that while consistent with their dreams, is essentially a scaled down version.

If we turn our attention to the right-hand side of Figure 7.1, we can see that while life has enabled the students' levels of social, human and financial capital to develop, there is no guarantee that it has done so in a direction that aligns to any particular vision they may hold. So while we most certainly have a more developed *general* social and human capital, any assumption that our students come ready to be entrepreneurs would be mistaken. The issue being that the value of any resource profile is idea dependent. Industry contacts and knowledge have the highest potential value in the domain in which they were developed, and a lower value elsewhere.

## AUDITING AND CREATING DEEP AWARENESS

To address this issue in a postgraduate context, I use two specific processes. As indicated in Figure 7.1, my students are starting from a different position vis-à-vis life experience and capability. My challenge is to ensure they are able to accurately define the nature of their vision, its resource requirements and the gap, if any, that exists. Unlike the undergraduate starting out with little to lose, my postgraduates have much to lose from being seduced by a long-held dream.

My postgraduate students typically have developed a strong set of values and these values quite often shape the nature of the visions they arrive in class with. Be they latent or already on the surface and looking for direction, or permission as the case may be. I approach the issue of their resource profile and related vision from an auditing process. The following chapter is the most expansive in the book. It outlines the sense-making process my students use to analyse their abilities vis-à-vis their vision and the environment within which they nominate to operate within. The nature of this auditing process will become more obvious as this sense-making process is explained. For now, we can just focus on the value gained from auditing a student's resource profile. My basic argument is that once a deep enough level of awareness is created around the importance of the nascent entrepreneur's resource profile we have then developed ability for an individual to plan appropriately.

I use classroom discussion and online tools to discuss the importance of one's resource profile. I ensure my students understand that assuming an individual will become a team and therefore any individual resource profile gaps will be filled in does not always play out that way. We discuss the pitfalls and opportunities of teams and partnerships. Typically, there are enough students who have business experience, partnership experience and/or close-hand observations of both to enable our feet to be grounded on such matters.

We develop case studies in the moment, identifying local identities known to them and try to explain their success or failure using their assumed resource profiles as the starting point. This is always an excellent way to get my students involved. More often than not I have no intimate knowledge of the local identity and therefore rely upon my students to create the case study. Before not too long, competing versions as to someone's success or otherwise become the topics of debate. I try to get the students to contemplate all the various accounts being suggested. Now entrepreneurship is the subject they hold the expertise in, I am merely the scribe and provocateur at large.

Having moved from the idea of the resource profile as a quaint theorectical idea to something around which they can express opinions, the opportunity to personalise the idea has arrived. I ask each of the students to address the class. For what do you hold a passion? What idea would allow you to act on your passions? To what extent do you hold a sufficient resource profile to act on this passion? To what extent do you feel motivated to act on this passion? The answers to these four questions ensure that my class, and therefore my students' learning, has truly begun. An assumed gap has been signalled between the current position of the student, their passions and the resource profile they claim to hold vis-à-vis their idea.

As our class progresses, the remaining elements of the sense-making framework are enfolded into their cognitive mixing bowls. My students leave me, having spent a couple of days having had the opportunity to express their passions and the ideas they believe might allow them to act upon them. They have been given a new set of eyes through which to see the world. They have been set the challenge of auditing their ability to become the lead actor in a play of their creation. When they again return to the classroom they report what they have learned from gathering information in their local communities.

It is at this point that they have determined the gap honestly or need some further help from some classroom probing. It is at this point that pennies start dropping and the reality of their situation starts to emerge. They either have the capacity to enact community level change, or, they don't have that capacity. Neither outcome, or the stuff in between is a problem; the key is being able to have foresight to know what the gap is at that point in time. To be able to make sound decisions at this point in time around such matters is critical. After this point in time, the application of the existing resource profile to the original idea or it's reorientation to other ideas can be contemplated or shelved. The key issue is that such decision-making has been sharpened and occurs with as many knowns known and as few unknowns unknown as humanly possible. Let us consider the importance that other educators place on the development of social and human capital.

## GLOBAL PERSPECTIVES

The importance of developing within our students a deep appreciation of their resource profile is clearly supported globally. Dr Susan Rushworth at the Swinburne University of Technology in Australia stressed that it is one of the key learning objectives for her students. Annette Naudin at Birmingham City University in England felt that students often don't recognise these values until it is pointed out to them. Thus, it is a critical part of the learning experience. For Peter Balan at the University of South Australia in Australia, this is what an entrepreneurship course is about, getting the students to understand the notion of *personal enterprise* and how they can draw on their own capabilities.

There was widespread agreement as to the importance of this issue across all aspects of our teaching. Monica Kreuger, President of Global Infobrokers in Canada argued that this is fundamental – all great ideas turn into reality through the work of many hands, not the work of a few. Incubator level work is often the purview of a few but then it needs to move to the next level and that requires suppliers, customers, competitors, funders, community, government etc. So in essence, as stated by Associate Professor Jonathan Lean at Plymouth University in England, our concern about this issue is very important, and part of the purpose of a postgraduate EE course is to enhance these. For Dr Bill Kirkley at Massey University in New Zealand, it is quite critical to self-efficacy and to building the self-confidence needed to venture out on their own.

However, I will leave the last word to Dr Elena Rodriguez-Falcon at Sheffield University in England who channels Lewis Carroll's (1869: 89) *Alice in Wonderland*. Alice asked to the Cheshire Cat, 'Would you tell me, please, which way I ought to walk from here?' 'That depends a good deal on where you want to get to,' said the Cat. 'I don't much care where,' said Alice. 'Then it doesn't matter which way you go,' said the Cat. Elena often comes back to this story, it tells her much about understanding your own goals, your vision, your ideals ... but also, where you are starting from; so postgraduate students and everyone else need to learn about their social and human capital.

## SUMMARY

The argument being made is that knowing one's resource profile relative to a particular idea is critical to making better decisions. To what extent are you ensuring your students understand the ramifications of making decisions in the absence all information germane to the circumstances of their thinking? The ideas discussed here are simple, but not always given sufficient elevation in the pecking order of topics placed within our curriculum. Hopefully, the value of such focus will be amply demonstrated in the following chapter.

# PART III

# Being Entrepreneurial

# 8.   Seeing the World Differently

> It is because men have been ignorant of the probable consequences, or have disregarded them, that human history presents such a picture of the devastation and waste of human energy and of the wreck of human hopes. If there is any salvation for the human race from the woe and misery it is in knowledge and in training to use knowledge. (Sumner, 1902: 73)

I am very fortunate to have so many students share with me their ideas on how they may create some form of new value in their communities. Many of the ideas I hear are not merely pipe dreams, something that someone would love to achieve if they only ever gained the opportunity. Quite often, students have come to a realisation that the time is nigh, that their motivation is in place and permissions have been granted for them to step forward and indulge an adventure. While I cannot see into the future with any more clarity than any other person, my life experience as an entrepreneur and an EE educator give me certain insights. Insights that raise concerns from time to time about just what is being risked and the extent to which I have encouraged any such contemplation. This chapter represents my response to ensuring my students have dotted as many i's and crossed as many t's as is possible within the time and other resource constraints they confront.

It is my intention to walk you methodically through this process. For this chapter is the heart and soul of the book. It is the primary contribution I seek to make. The preceding chapters have laid the groundwork for the thinking that has accompanied the development of this framework. My confidence in this framework is buoyed by hundreds of students experiencing it and acknowledging the new view of the world they have developed. I will make no outrageous claims that the use of this framework will increase the success rate for any start-up; for I do not wish to contradict my early statements regarding the separation of purpose and consequences. I merely state my confidence that the framework I will introduce you to will enable students to advance their understanding of the factors that will undoubtedly influence the success or otherwise of the efforts to create new value. Rather than asking questions of you the reader towards the end of the chapter, as is my usual practice, I will undertake to ask you a host of questions as proceed through

*Being entrepreneurial*

the different sections of the framework. I will also endeavour to supply examples related to each stage so that the framework's components can fit together in your mind as well.

Whilst the last component of this framework is the process of emergy, it is important that I draw attention to it at this point in time to alert you of its significant importance. The concept of emergy was developed by Odum (1995) and is defined as available (or stored) energy of one kind previously required directly and indirectly to make a product or service that can be converted into useful energy by other entities within an ecosystem. It is for all intentions a form of invisible energy that can be expected to influence the success or otherwise of entrepreneurs' efforts. The framework explicitly seeks to create the cognitive powers to see this invisible energy and to use it productively where possible. So while many of the components of the framework are well known and accepted, several are concepts drafted in from the domain of ecology, hence the title of environment interaction framework. Together, I believe they make this framework innovative and useful for both educator and student.

## THE ENVIRONMENTAL INTERACTION FRAMEWORK

### The Idea

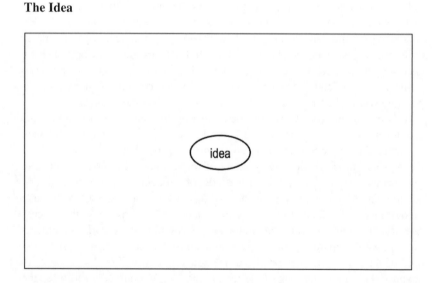

*Figure 8.1    The idea*

Ideas are the lifeblood of social change. Entrepreneurs have ideas that challenge the status quo and thus are agents of social change. My discussion of the environmental interaction begins with the emergence of an idea (see Figure 8.1 above). Perhaps an idea related to profit-oriented motives or more altruistically conceived. The constant supply of ideas into a society provides the starting point of the framework. However, the framework is less concerned with ideas in aggregate than it is with individual ideas.

## The Resource Profile

The idea a student voices is not merely an idea in isolation; it is an initial artefact of a potential agent of change. A dialogic relationship (Bruyat and Julien, 2001) exists between the idea's conceiver and the idea itself. This is highlighted in Figure 8.2 below with the addition of the notations SC, HC and FC, which account for the student's social, human and financial capital.

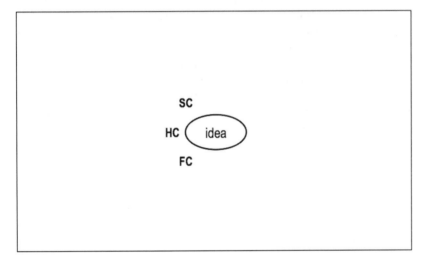

*Figure 8.2   The dialogic relationship between student and idea*

Essentially, the idea cannot exist in a vacuum, as the agent of change cannot without an idea. As discussed in the previous chapter, the first concern for the student is the extent of social relations they currently hold that would aid their future development of the idea. Just who should be known to advance the student's participation in championing the idea? To the extent that the student knows persons assumed to be able to contribute to the idea's development, how well are they known? Could they be relied upon to assist the student? Could they introduce the student to other important persons? Could they be willing to also become involved in the idea's development?

The student's next concern relates to what particular knowledge and/or expertise would be required to develop the idea? That is, what type of human capital would be necessary to develop the idea? If the student doesn't have the required expertise, might their social capital provide access to it? Or, might such expertise be relatively easy to acquire regardless? How many resources might need to be acquired to move this idea forward? Would the student be expected to be able to gain access to any such resources? Or, stated another way, do they have sufficient financial capital to move forward in championing this idea?

One can easily imagine a bank employee taking a redundancy payment and looking to establish an independent financial services business. Having been trained by his or her past employer and gained the accreditation to practice in the industry, they would be well set to exploit the social contacts cultivated naturally whilst an employee in the industry. Alternatively, consider the boilermaker welder who has always dreamed of opening a bakery so that he can share his grandmother's various tried and true recipes. Lacking any trade background training in his chosen industry, and not knowing any industry contacts, he may well struggle.

The initial questions at this stage are relatively simple. Is there sufficient alignment of the student's (and/or their team's) social human and financial capitals to consider their idea feasible at this point in time? If not, can these deficiencies be overcome easily? Assuming the answer is yes, lets move along to the next stage of the framework.

**Cognitive and Socio-Political Legitimacy**

Independent of the student's thinking and their resource profile, some degree of legitimacy most likely exists in relation to their idea. In Figure 8.3 below, both cognitive and socio-political legitimacy have been added to the framework. Two issues concern the student at this stage of their evaluation. First, is a concern for the extent to which the features and/or underlying philosophies of their idea are known within their community? That is, does their idea already have cognitive legitimacy, and if so, by whom and how many? To the extent that their idea already has that taken for granted status in society (Aldrich, 1999), they may be onto a winner. Alternatively, perhaps while society knows about it, perhaps important sections of society disapprove of the idea. Perhaps worse still, it is illegal or controversial in terms of its future development.

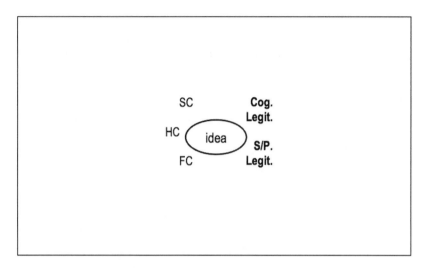

*Figure 8.3    The legitimacy of the idea*

Consider a young couple that wish to open a bungee jumping operation at a scenic location frequented by many adventurous white-water rafters. Lets assume that collectively they have a sound resource profile having worked in similar tourist ventures overseas and being actively involved in the adventure tourism industry. Lets assume that finance and access to a physical location are also not a problem, so far so good.

In terms of legitimacy, they have zero problems with cognitive legitimacy. As an activity, bungee jumping is well known and a reasonable level of their local community has either jumped elsewhere or indicated they would be willing to give it a try. However, in their local community, bungee jumping is considered very high risk by certain stakeholders, essentially it lacks socio-political legitimacy. Consequently, it is not possible to gain permits/licences to operate such a business, despite the likelihood of consumer demand.

At this stage, several questions emerge that need careful consideration. Consider an idea that has both cognitive and socio-political legitimacy, this is good news, and on the basis that a suitable resource profile is available, other questions surrounding these issues will emerge as we get deeper into the framework. Alternatively, consider an idea like the bungee jumping example. While they don't have to educate the consumer as to what the service is, they do need to expend potentially considerable energy trying to gain regulatory support. Do they have the sufficient resource to invest into such potentially time consuming activities? Or, switch things around, they have socio-political legitimacy but little if cognitive legitimacy exists. How much will it cost in time and/or money to educate the potential consumer about the nature of the service? Might they be trying to develop primary demand for a new and novel service, or selective demand for a competing service? If their budget is tight, can they afford to attempt to do this? Finally, consider the case where neither form of legitimacy exists. Can they even try to educate the public when there is no guarantee that the service will ever exist? Given the cash-strapped nature of most start-ups, we need to ensure our students are asking these questions. The next component of the framework is the external environment.

## The External Environment

Ideas always exist in a context. Legitimacy is a property of a local and/or external environment. We must ensure that the properties of the environment are fully understood as most processes contained within the framework operate in sync with the other properties of the environment.

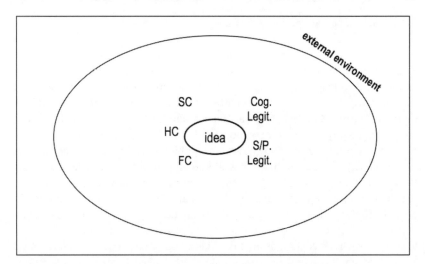

*Figure 8.4   The external environment*

With reference to Brandon's (1990) conception of the dimensions of the environment, we can consider the external environment. The external environment consists of all elements and factors that could reasonably be expected to influence the development of the idea. Whilst this overarching view of the environment does little to highlight which factors are of most importance to one idea or another, it is nevertheless very important. Students must understand that the environment that we so often speak of so casually can be viewed at macro and micro levels. In this instance, we need for our students to be mindful of broad trends, for example, high interest rates that can influence many initiatives in society. It is also important that the student starts to make a connection between what factors in a community relate to the properties of the external environment that impact the degree of legitimacy that may exist for any given idea.

## The Selective and Ecological Environments

Next, Brandon (1990) identifies a second dimension of the environment as the *ecological* environment, which refers to a narrowing down of focus, as illustrated in Figure 8.5 below. Now we are only concerned with those factors that specifically contribute to developing a specific idea. This could be the availability of any specific resources important in the idea's development. The third and last form of environment is the *selective* environment. The selective environment refers to those factors of the external environment that would specifically determine the differential fitness of any aspect of the idea's assumed interacting elements.

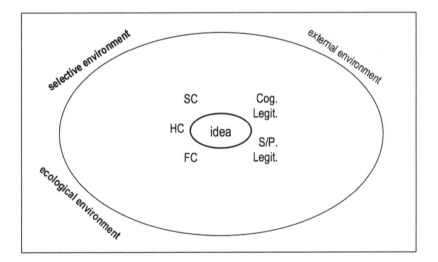

*Figure 8.5 The selective and ecological environments*

Under such a proposal, the *general* environment can exist independently of an idea, and aspects of it can be altered by other ideas, without any positive or negative impact on the nature of selection. However, the *selective* environment has no existence independent of the idea; it represents the actual *niche* of the idea. Once the dimensions of a given environment can be accounted for, the ability of one or more ideas/initiatives to alter these dimensions can be considered.

Returning to the example of our boilermaker welder and his proposed bakery, assuming he has sorted out his resource profile, understanding the selective and ecological environment will be of great importance. In this example we need to consider which resources a bakery most needs from its ecological environment. Two come to mind. First, to be able to operate, they will need skilled staff. Assuming there is a reliable supply of qualified people, the next resource is money. The money must come from customers. Let's assume he intends to operate in the suburb, Poorville. In Poorville, income levels are very low and most locals buy their bakery products from the major supermarkets that sell cheap affordable bakery products. So while the ecological environment can supply some of the required resources, the negative influence of the selective environment may be too overpowering in this example.

Alternatively, if our boilermaker changed from a bakery to a bottle shop, things might look better. Now there is less reliance upon the ecological environment because any staff need not be qualified with a specific trade. Given that a disproportionate amount of the incomes of the locals in Poorville are spent on alcohol, the selective environment will be not as difficult to overcome. However, many locals disapprove of new bottle shops entering Poorville and this has led to less socio-political legitimacy around the nature of this idea.

A better way of overcoming these issues may be to think of relocating the proposed bakery to the neighbouring suburb of Richville. There, higher income levels are common. There is still access to plenty of qualified staff and the locals tend to ignore the inferior quality bakery products from the major supermarkets. Leaving competition aside at this stage, the selective and ecological environments both look supportive of the idea.

Once we open our students' eyes to the various positives and negatives of the selective and ecological environments that relate to their specific idea, many questions arise. We need to ensure our students' eyes are lowered to consider what actual success factors are available and what factors are potentially working against the idea. If we ask our students to consider the places where other similar ideas have worked and/or failed, we can invite many questions. Why do we think someone has failed or succeeded? Are there resource shortages common to this idea? Are the community perception issues related to the idea? Are there legal issues related to the idea? Are there competition or resource sharing issues related to the idea? Drawing our students toward a consideration of such questions requires them to develop an understanding of the process of social change. This is the next stage of the model that our students need to master. When all is said and done, all change can be reduced to the three elements of the evolutionary approach.

## The Process of Variation, Selection and Retention

In recent times, Aldrich (1999) has championed the use of an evolutionary approach through which to enable scholars of entrepreneurship to explain change. In Figure 8.6 below, the process of variation, selection and retention (VSR) is placed within the space of the environment. This placement signifies the central role that these three processes play at the intersection of the factors present in the external, ecological and selective environments.

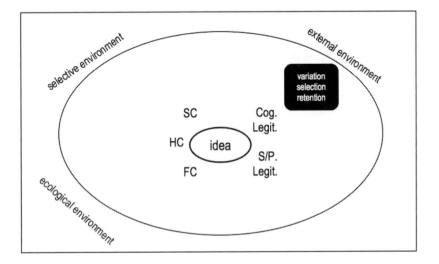

*Figure 8.6   The evolutionary approach*

The challenge for the students is to widen their appreciation of the contributing factors that ultimately relate to the process of social change. Let us first consider each of the VSR processes. Variations can be considered as any change from the current norm. Unfortunately, many researchers assume that the norms of any specific practice can be quite widespread, arguing that certain established ways of organising activities have achieved cognitive legitimacy with an industry. I tend to disagree, arguing alternatively that the level of diversity of organising activities found is merely a mirroring of the variability of the selective and ecological environments related to any of the students' ideas.

This is a very important point to consider your position on. It is widely accepted that competing ideas and/or organisational forms are selected for or against within a common environment. Once we move away from a view that the environment and its contents should be accounted for in terms of the macro level of the *external* environment, as discussed above, we expose ourselves to increased levels of environmental variation. If we accept that each idea has a *selective* environment that has no existence independent of that specific idea we have radically changed our conceptualisation of the environment. We have in fact moved to a place in which the notion of selective neighbourhoods (Brandon, 1996) makes perfect sense. Now we are only concerned with the relative fitness of an idea within a given set of parameters that ultimately contribute to the success of otherwise of the idea. For example, if our boilermaker welder was to establish his bakery in Poorville rather than in Richville, his eventual success would be most likely explainable by environmental factors rather than any consideration of the variation in his idea vis-à-vis other similar ideas. I will further explain this idea when the notion of selection is addressed.

Until then, let us continue our thinking around the idea of what variations are. Viewed as changes from the norm, variations can be seen to occur intentionally or through blind or accidental processes (Aldrich, 1999). So we accept that through human agency we can search for different ways to achieve any given way of organising an activity. This can be considered an intentional variation. Such processes can be inspired by pressure from the selective environment or perceptions about opportunities in the ecological or external environments. Alternatively, and potentially independent of the environmental or selection pressures, fortuitous events may see the emergence and/or awareness of new ways in which we may approach a situation. The relationship between variation and selection be they intentional or blind, is complex.

I suspect my explanation of this complexity is more complex than most due to my treatment of the environment and its dimensions. However, there are no apologies for any initial steeper learning as the eventual view afforded is significantly clearer and of more value to my students. To explain my different approach it is important to briefly state my philosophical position vis-à-vis my approach to using ecological and evolutionary concepts and theories. My approach is consistent with autecology and thus, I define the environment differently from more mainstream approaches such as Hannan and Freeman's (1977) organisational ecology (or population and community ecology). From an autecological approach, it is the idea (or firm) and its relations with the environment that of most interest. So, the idea (or firm) is not seen as merely an entity within a hierarchy. I therefore see each proposed idea (or firm) as potentially being 'adapted to a particular subset of the environmental circumstances that prevail within any locality' (Walter, 2013: 342). I also hold open the possibility that an idea (or firm) can influence any such particular subset in ways to increase its eventual fitness. I readily admit that my approach is very uncommon, but hold that it is consistent with such ideas in mainstream ecology and that ultimately, this is what makes it so potentially useful to my students. Let us now return to the issue of selection.

From the simplest perspective, Aldrich (1999) notes that selection can occur through external or internal processes. So we can imagine that the lack of socio-political legitimacy could constitute an external process of selection, something that may lie beyond the control of the student. Alternatively, having sensed that there may be issues regarding securing socio-political legitimacy, the proponent of the idea may seek to arrange their activities in such a way to overcome any such problems. Now it is the proponent internally selecting for a specific approach, presumably from a given set of possible variations.

A key issue from the perspective of an idea (or firm) is; (1) are very similar ideas (or firms) operating and interacting in a common environment? That is, do they share common external, ecological and selective environments? If the answer is yes than the more traditional process of natural selection is a logical approach. We can assume that the environment will do an indiscriminate job of sorting the fit from the less fit. However, if the answer is no (i.e. because we incorrectly assume they (a) are similar, (b) interact and (c) experience a common environment, or we know this not to be true), then environmental selection provides a valid means to explain the actual fitness of a single idea (or firm) and/or other surrounding/related ideas (or firms).

This approach actually makes the student's life much easier. Trying to understand all manner of factors present in the external environment is almost impossible; yet we commonly ask this of students. Once we can zero in on the potential fitness of a given idea and the specific nature of its ecological and selective environments we provide a clean space for our students to develop and test their assumptions. In this thinking space students can get closer to understanding how the process of external selection is operating and how they might be able to counter such external pressure.

Despite recognition that the process of selection can be viewed as operating in a variety of complex ways (see Amburgey, Dacin and Kelly, 1994), very little advancement has been made to investigate this (although see Jones, 2007). Ignoring the reality that selection can be seen to occur in various observable patterns does our students a disservice. All too frequently selection is cast as force that acts to stabilize (or preserve) specific factors that aid the fitness of entities in a population. While it is true that we can think of *stabilizing* selection performing such a function, selection may also work in *directional* and *disruptive* ways. Indeed, for our students to appreciate the way in which selection is present in the local environment to which their thinking is being applied, they must fully understand all three processes. They must also appreciate the likely combinations the three processes. Understanding which external forces are present or likely to be present in a local environment is critically important to any nascent entrepreneur. Such knowledge contributes to the eventual decision-making about which variations to select internally for and which existing methods of organisation to preserve with.

The last component of the VSR process is the mechanism of retention. Aldrich (1999: 30) argues that 'retention occurs when selected variations are preserved, duplicated, or otherwise reproduced' to ensure their repetitive use. Most commentators of the VSR approach also highlight the importance of the struggle for resources that continually surrounds the entrepreneurs' decision-making. I prefer not to lead my students towards this way of thinking. It has the potential to put the VSR processes into the realm of black-box processes. Once students can envisage the actual nature of the selective and ecological environments for their ideas that tend to sidestep many of the challenges of this issue.

Lets again consider the bank employee taking a redundancy payment and looking to establish an independent financial services business. He or she will most likely have been exposed to many operating formats in the financial services industry, although a true understanding may not be possible from afar. Nevertheless, their planning will lead them to consider various ways to operate. Perhaps the underlying trends with regards to regulation will be of specific importance. In this instance, normal stabilizing selection processes would be insufficient. This is an industry in which best practice is forever emerging based on the external controls of regulators. External selection is typically operating in a directional manner in terms of increasing accountability. So consideration of external variations needs to factor in the direction of the prevailing direction selection is taking, especially if a long-term approach is being undertaken.

However, ultimately it will be the ability of the new venture to attract specific resources that will matter. Simply adopting the practices apparently favoured within an industry will not ensure survival. As a fledging start-up, the most important resource is income. The principle's social capital will be of critical importance in this respect. To the extent that the principle can use his or her human capital and social networks to access initial income, they will most likely succeed in the short-term. However, in the long-term, the venture will require deeper levels of engagement and exploitation of the ecological environment to succeed. Thus, selection for or against the start-up will be based on the fit between the venture and its ability to acquire income streams from its ecological environment more so than the actual natural of what types of activities are by and large assumed to be favoured by the external environment.

This process of thinking requires of our students a far deeper level an analysis and insight than most normal approaches. Frequently when the processes of VSR are discussed, it is assumed that an evolutionary process is being referred to. While that is correct, what is more important for the student to understand is that any such process is being driven by complex ecological processes. It is these processes that our students need to understand. Can our students connect the dots that join the presence or otherwise of legitimacy for their idea? Can they see the importance of one's resource profile in being able to exploit the actual ecological environment related to their idea? Is the student able to discern between selection for various forms or organisation or practice and actual factors that would specifically work for or against their actual idea? This is the real crux of it. Being able to move the students beyond unexplored assumptions to actual critical thinking about how selection is and might be present.

**The Process of Value Creation**

The next addition to the framework is the processes of value creation. As highlighted in Figure 8.7 below, three processes are suggested; the value chain, the value shop and the value network (Stabell and Fjeldstad, 1998). Exposing our students' thinking to these three value creation logics is important to enabling them to 1) envisage how they will create value, and 2) ensuring they comprehend the relationship between selection for or against and the processes of creating value.

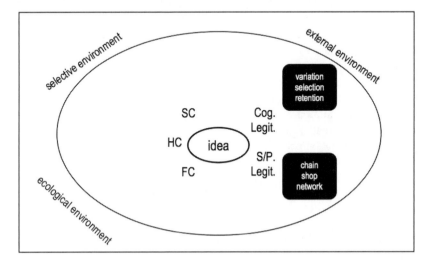

*Figure 8.7 Value creation processes*

I observe that quite frequently the value chain logic is defaulted to when the process of value creation is discussed. While this may be perfectly appropriate for a good many ideas, it is also most inappropriate for an increasing number of ideas our students contemplate. Our students increasing contemplate action in online worlds and via superior service delivery. To fully appreciate the availability of resources and the nature of selection likely it is important our students know these three value creation logics. Put simply, are our student transforming a lesser resource into a higher value resource? Are they allocating resources in unique ways to satisfy the unique individual requirements of a specific customer/opportunity? Are they exploiting network relationships by using a mediating technology? Perhaps they are employing a combination or all three of these approaches to create value.

Once our students can visualise the processes through which they plan to create and capture value, they can also understand the primary activities required to do so. They can envisage the key cost and value drivers along with the nature of organisational structures required to support such drivers. Armed with such insight, students are able to further examine the nature of the selective and ecological environments. This is the true nature of the framework; it is like peeling layers off an onion. The further the students are drawn into the frameworks elements, the more clarity around each component develops.

Let us return to the boilermaker welder and his desire to operate a bakery. There is no doubt Porter's (1985) value chain logic will serve him well. Alternatively, the value shop approach of Stabell and Fjeldstad (1998) will also be required to offer individual services that satisfy the diverse needs of any such customer base. What about a student who wishes to start an online travel agency? They will need to customise service and product offerings and exploit the nature of the online business environment, so a combination of value shop and value network processes.

What is important is that our students are able to state how they believe they will create and capture value. Our challenge is to get them to explore further how in reality this may actually occur. Once we can move our students' thinking into this space, we succeed in getting them to view the operation of their idea from the end-user's perspective. This is important as it again sharpens focus on the processes of selection, for and against their idea.

The next component of the framework (see Figure 8.8) relates to opening our students' minds to the positive and negative interrelationships that significantly shape the nature of the environments they will encounter/shape. It has been noted that the most important attributes of a system are the regular interactions (Lidicker, 1979), or coactions, as they will be referred to here.

## Accounting for coactions

In his seminal paper on coaction theory, Haskell (1949: 46) claimed that in any activity occurring in society, 'there are diversely powerful individuals which can be separated in two groups or classes, the weak and the strong'. Further, that 'these two main classes can have nine, and only nine, qualitatively different relations towards each other'. Lastly, he noted that 'the major properties of societies vary with coaction'. I know that when my students can comprehend the nature of interactions that may be expected to exist vis-à-vis their idea's operation, they have uncovered another level of valuable thinking.

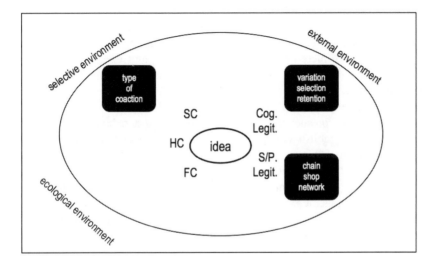

*Figure 8.8   Type of coaction*

Encouraging students to view themselves as either strong or weak in relation to other aspects of society is beneficial to their thinking. It increases the likelihood that they will contemplate more processes of selection than may likely occur. It increases the likelihood that they will consider who controls the nature of the resources they require. It encourages them to contemplate who is best placed to influence/create legitimacy for related aspects of their idea. The first starting point is to consider the types of relations possible. There are various types of relations in which positive outcomes are possible for either or both the weak and strong.

Let us assume two entities 'A' and 'B'. The relations between 'A' and 'B' can be categorised as containing negative (-), positive (+) and neutral (o) outcomes. With the outcomes for 'A' illustrated on the left-hand side, and 'B' on the right-hand side, we can have the following outcomes where 'A' always has a negative outcome: -/-, -/o, or -/+. Alternatively, 'A' may receive the following positive outcomes: +/-, +/o, or +/+. The remaining three types of outcomes would be o/-, o/o, or o/+. So while there are three possible types of interaction between 'A' and 'B' in which 'A' receives positive outcomes, there are six in which 'A' doesn't, and vice versa for 'B'.

Ensuring students contemplate such a range of interactions allows the nature of the ecosystem into which they see their ideas playing out to become more transparent. Importantly, it also allows them to understand the extent to which their ideas might also change aspects of the selective and ecological environment. This process, known as niche construction (Odling-Smee, Laland and Feldman, 2003) requires the students to look beyond to how selection might work for or against them. They need to also consider how their individual actions may, over time, produce changes in the environment. For example, the mere presence of a particular type of operation may over time change the nature of socio-political legitimacy experienced. Therefore, it is important students understand how their actions may influence the potential nature of selection processes experienced over time.

Let us again consider the bank employee taking a redundancy payment and looking to establish an independent financial services business. He or she may struggle to achieve cognitive legitimacy at the time of commencing operations. At that very moment in time, selection is working against he or she, with potential and important initial incomes limited. However, over time, their engagement with local factors in the community, such as sponsoring local sporting clubs on the basis on any patronage from members of a particular club can change the nature of selection, and importantly, the nature of coaction.

When the financial services business began, the nature of coaction between it and the assumed local sporting club was o/o. Neither entity was affected negatively or positively by the presence of each other in the local community. The offer to provide the sporting club with a financial reward if its members used the financial services business for their insurances and investments in exchange for signage around the sporting club's premises changed the nature of coaction. At that moment in time, a commensalistic relation (o/+) had started to occur, within which the host sporting club was unaffected, whilst the financial services business gained benefits from the signage. Hopefully, as the relationship continues, a symbiotic relationship (+/+) would emerge whereby both entities gain from the relationship as members of the sporting club become users of the financial services business and they return financial support to the sporting club. The power from this type of thinking is that my students become strategic in their conceptualisation about the nature of interaction that may occur between their idea and the environment they will encounter/create.

## The Strategic Orientation

The next component of the framework relates to how this strategic thinking manifests itself into the structures and positioning required to best support their idea. In Figure 8.9 attention is drawn to r and K strategies and the issue of specialisation or generalising.

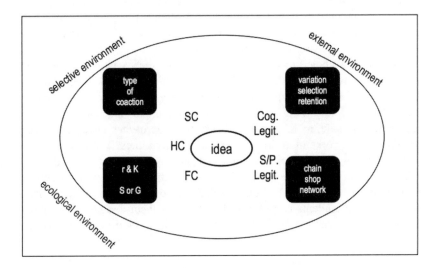

*Figure 8.9 Strategic orientation*

Once students accept that the nature of selection will vary over time and with different forms of coaction, they can plan accordingly. They can understand the nature of risk inherent in starting something that lacks cognitive and/or socio-political legitimacy. They can sense what resources are available and which are not. They can understand how strong or weak their resource profile is. They can sense the sense of direction and power of selection in the environment. Sadly, academics have reduced the complexity of our world by encouraging nascent entrepreneurs to view the attractiveness of the environment using Porter's (1980) five forces model or categorising resources into valuable and rare. These tools all have a potential value if employed correctly, sadly that occurs too infrequently.

At the risk of offering yet another set of typologies for my students to use and therefore joining the ranks of those that seek to demystify the complexity of the environment, I offer this explanation. In the above paragraph I have alluded to a range of factors I feel my students have discerned about the environment they may encounter. That is, I have ensured their familiarity with such matters is more than cursory. It is only once that they have been forced through such mental and exploratory gymnastics that issues related to strategy are broached.

Therefore, my students become aware of several strategic choices, choices that assume the possibility of better aligning structure and strategy with a concern for the environment. Notice, I am not assuming they are held captive to the environment's forces, nor capable of plotting a way to overcome such forces. I am helping them to become aware of the likely nature of interaction between themselves, the environments they interact with, including other entities that may be stronger or weaker than them.

They have a choice to commit themselves in such a way that they can potentially minimise their losses if things don't go as planned. This is referred to as an 'r' strategy. Alternatively, they have a choice to commit themselves for the long-term, perhaps seeking to take advantage of economies of scale, a 'K' strategy. These two approaches have been made popular by the works of Aldrich (1999) and many others. These ideas build on the initial work of MacArthur and Wilson (1967) who observed that the natural disposition of some entities in nature predisposed them under certain environmental conditions to hold a selection advantage. Introducing such thinking to our students is useful in that it allows them to again think about the forces of selection and to attempt to match their structure to the environment.

The 'r' strategist is typically opportunistic, staying nimble, trying to sense the way forward in an environment subject to sudden and potentially unpredictable change. Thus, the 'r' strategist adopts a short-term outlook, perhaps leasing rather than buying, perhaps working with scaled up prototypes rather mature products. Alternatively, the 'K' strategist seeks the surety that comes from exploiting economies of scale, of financing over the long-term, and operating in more assumed stable environments. Determining which strategic orientation should be used is confounded by the reality that many firms adopt both strategies within various aspects of the operations. It is quite expected that a 'r' strategist will evolve into a 'K' strategist as industries mature and environments become more predictable.

Our next concern is with the degree to which we see our student's offering appealing to a broad audience or a narrow audience. The choice to specialise or generalise also is connected to the extent to which our chosen industry is emerging or already established. To the extent that it is still emerging and consumer preferences are yet to become obvious, being a generalist make sense. However, if we know what consumers want and if selection already favours 'K' strategists, then being a specialist may make more sense. One of the challenges in our students' thinking in this regard is not to fall into the trap of assuming that because other firms appear to be selected for by the environment, they might be too. In reality, our students may not be able to replicate the types of coactions they experience. They may also operate with radically different selective and ecological environments. They may hold positions of strength in their environments vis-à-vis our students' likely position. The key issue is to understand how selection forces and resource availability/exploitation will differ if we offer a product (and/or products) to a wider audience than if we were to offer a product (and/or products) to a narrower audience.

Let us return to the example of our boilermaker welder and his proposed bakery, again assuming he has made sense of all of the other issues raised above. He will face the option of leasing a bakery, buying a bakery or even building a bakery. Clearly leasing a bakery as an 'r' strategist would carry less risk. The business would have a track record that should provide some surety about its expected performance. Alternatively, he could buy an existing bakery as a 'K' strategist, committing himself to a long-term schedule of loan payments. In conjunction with that decision will be a determination on how best to allocate resources. Might it be best to specialise in wedding cakes or be a generalist an offer all forms of bakery products? Again, the importance of understanding the selective and ecological environments looms large. How many weddings are there in the region that could be expected to consider his bakery for a wedding cake? How many other bakeries act as generalist?

By now we have developed with our students a capacity for asking questions that are not normally found in textbooks where prescriptive processes are given most attention. While we have not dealt with the issues of luck, good or bad, in any detail, I have come to the conclusion that the next component of the framework tends to retrospectively explain both forms of luck. Indeed, many of the decision-making challenges that have emerged above can now be revisited through the introduction of the next component of the framework.

## Emergy

The idea of emergy is without the most powerful concepts that my students need to grasp. For once it is understood, my students have a capacity to see their world in an entirely new way. Comprehension of this component removes a large degree of potential ignorance, and opens the way for an exciting new process of opportunistic speculation. Emergy can be thought of as types of energy directly and/or indirectly used in creation of a resource, product of service (Odum, 1995). In Figure 8.10 below, an arrow moves from left to right signifying the presence of energy that while independent of any student's initial idea, will ultimately be present in any explanation of the nature of selection operating on the student's idea.

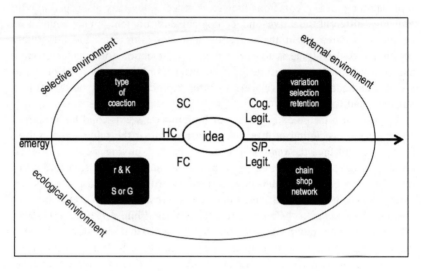

*Figure 8.10   Accounting for emergy*

Entrepreneurs do not and cannot control all the resources that ultimately determine their futures. That is why luck is never far from an explanation of success or failure. Entrepreneurs merely seek to exploit what resources are available, regardless of ownership. Borrowing from the ecological literature, I ensure my students understand the importance of ecological versatility (Mac Nally, 1995: 19), or 'the degree to which ... [firms] ... can fully exploit resources in their local environment'.

I am yet to meet a student who could not identify sources of emergy related to their idea. But I rarely meet students who are already aware of such freely available energy. This is why the idea of emergy is so powerful. To fully explain this idea the use of some actual examples will assist. I have been researching the survival of pizzerias in the restaurant industry for several years. What became obvious very quickly is that the survival of many pizzerias is determined by factors beyond their control; but factors nevertheless that they can exploit.

Since the emergence of the large and powerful franchised pizza chains, constant pulses of energy have been transmitted into western households on a daily basis through the use of television advertising. So, powerful firms, geographically    spread    throughout    global    landscapes    use    television advertising to draw in the resource they most require; consumer dollars. Unlike the local independent pizzerias, the franchised pizzerias have a business model built upon the need for very high levels of turnover to satisfy their low operating margins. Put simply, metaphorically, the metabolism of a franchised pizzeria is faster than the local independent pizzeria. The franchised pizzeria must consume more resources in order to survive, that is they must achieve significantly higher levels of turnover. To achieve this they must commit higher than normal levels of energy to forage; or to advertise.

In terms of our previous discussion on coaction relations, the franchised pizzerias are the strong and the local independent the weak. However, because of the niche constructing activities of the franchised pizzeria, quite frequently the ecological and selective environments of the local pizzerias are altered in favourable ways. Essentially, primary demand for pizza is increased across the community to the benefit of all, especially the local independent pizzerias who have not had to expend energy to acquire consumer dollars; they merely had to exploit the available resources. This is a classic commensalistic coaction (o/+) whereby the strong is unaffected by the presence of the weak, but the weak gains a specific benefit from the presence of the strong.

Once students understand the idea that other entities are contributing energy into the external environment, and that sometimes this energy directly influences the selective and ecological environment of their specific idea, they can see their world quite differently. They begin to step back and ask how they can exploit the environment, much like a surfer considering which beach to use to access the best waves. Rather than assuming that they may be locked in a battle to the death with bigger and stronger entities, they see the opportunity to co-exist alongside such entities. Or perhaps to locate their operations out of harm's way, yet still close enough to benefit from the available emergy. In the example used above, this makes sense as the nature of advertising from the larger franchised operators is very predictable, it is their sole means of survival.

## Other Predictable Sources of Emergy

There are two other sources of emergy that can be quite easily found. As indicated in Figure 8.11, our students can be alert to top-down government interventions and also bottom-up community driven interventions. It is quite amazing how often when discussing an idea with a student or colleague that no mention is made of the opportunity to tap into top-down or bottom-up initiatives. In many instances such initiatives may be only short-lived, but they may provide specific assistance to our students' ideas in terms of

ensuring adequate cognitive or socio-political legitimacy. It may therefore
ensure that the ecological environment is sufficiently primed to favour the
nascent entrepreneur's activities. Or, perhaps the edge will be taken off the
selective environment. Let us consider an example.

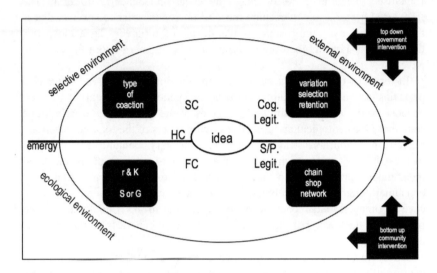

*Figure 8.11    Other sources of emergy*

Returning again to our bank employee taking a redundancy payment and
looking to establish an independent financial services business, how might he
or she find emergy? Well let's suppose the government is concerned about
financial literacy, and they decide to sponsor some year-long programs that
offer free education about such matters to adolescent youth. Such a program
may ensure the financial services business has its initial costs covered during
the period when other resources are being committed to developing a brand
in the local community. Indeed, the fact that the business is delivering such a
service on behalf of the government lends socio-political legitimacy to the
entity. The key here is to be aware of such programs, to actually be looking
for such initiatives to attach the business to in the short-term.

Let's also return to our boilermaker welder and his proposed bakery.
Many community groups are springing up that seek to provide information
and resources for people suffering from celiac disease, or intolerance to
gluten. What if our new bakery was to work closely with such groups and
specialise in gluten free products? He may be able to develop a reputation
and wholesale gluten free products to other local bakeries not willing to cater
to this segment of the market. In this way, he might be able to exploit what

was a negative aspect of the selective environment through tapping into a growing bottom-up intervention. So, there we are, a framework that while simple in design holds the possibility of radically changing the way our students' see their surrounds. Perhaps now it is appropriate to consider the views of my students who have experienced this approach in thinking. One aspect that hasn't yet been discussed is how to operationalise the process.

## Giving More Than One Set of Glasses

A key aspect of the sense-making process is not simply the process of moving through each additional component. What seems to really make the process come to life is through *workshopping* each student's thinking. I deliberately seek to have a group discussion of each student's judgement. This provides space for other members of the class to add to their judgement by lending ideas and perhaps even providing suggestions of how to improve one's resource profile or how to improve overall legitimacy. What also happens through this process is that where some aspect of the process may have been overlooked, or misunderstood, this process of group discussion fills in the gaps. It also provides an opportunity for the students to become the focus of everyone's' attention, thereby increasing the responsibility upon each student to prepare for their moment in the sun. They tend to thrive on the opportunity to share their thinking knowing that many other sets of eyes will now consider the nature of their opportunity.

When I reflect upon the comments students have shared with me about the value of the sense-making process I see several things. First, I see that the process helps them to make sense of how their idea might play out in reality. Second, I see the confidence it brings to their thinking. Third, I see the organisation it brings to their thinking so that they know what is expected of them. Lastly, I see many students using process in evaluative situations that lay beyond their graduation. Many of these sentiments are captured in the student comments below.

> As an adult learner, the knowledge I have most readily acquired and indeed retained has been that which was provided to me through a sense-making framework – that which was taught to me in a manner that enabled my referencing of the knowledge to concepts relevant to my life and experiences, which in turn legitimised the new-found knowledge for me. (student comment no. 1)

> I liked the model Colin used to help us understand the implications of the wider influences on our decision-making, and the way we could frame our research project through it. (student comment no. 2)

The sense-making framework was of benefit because it showed us you can take any idea and consider it via a framework to see if the idea has legs. It shows the strengths and weaknesses of the idea. (student comment no. 3)

I use this approach when assessing the viability of a number of initiatives at my current job. Whether they are fundraising initiatives or development projects in Southern Africa, assessing the market and the legitimacy of an idea are extremely important! (student comment no. 4)

To see the big picture and the possibilities within this framework has allowed me to follow up and bring to fruition a particular idea/project. (student comment no. 5)

I strongly believe that your approach provided me with access to a sense-making framework. I am better able to *see* what needs to change, assess, compare and contrast possible solutions and use what I have to make that change. (student comment no. 6)

The sense-making framework provided an over-arching guideline in which the learning and academic development could take place. This benefited us as learners because it gave a clear indication of requirements and structure as related to the learning outcomes. (student comment no. 7)

Colin's approach to examining an idea or an issue provided a strong framework for sense and decision making. This has provided great benefits already with regard to me having a better approach to examining business opportunities and challenges by mapping the resources I have and need. (student comment no. 8)

Colin was able to ask questions of an individual presenting or trying to sell an idea that made them reassess a potential critical aspect of an idea in a manner that was not degrading or embarrassing to the individual, but rather created a light bulb moment for the group and class. (student comment no. 9)

For me this remains an essential framework to interpret any situation I have needed to analyse, and I have used it in my practice many times since it was introduced to me. (student comment no. 10)

You encouraged students to question their interpretation of a situation relative to the opinion of others and I believe the way you approached this gave students greater respect (and tolerance) for the opinions of others. (student comment no. 11)

## Seeing the World Differently

A key issue here is not whether there is a right way to work with your students in this regard, but whether your students see you as an authority of the approach you support. For it is in you and your stewardship of their learning that that seek assurance. I see a weakness for educators of EE who uses an approach to sense-making that they don't truly believe in. Students know when you believe in something and when you just borrowing an idea to occupy their thinking for a class or two. My students engage with my framework prior to us meeting for the first time. And they use it continuously thereafter. I demonstrate my commitment to the framework and to they're learning outcomes by staying on song throughout the process.

## GLOBAL PERSPECTIVES

From the range of response to the IE-II Survey I can sense that discussion between students is an important element of many sense-making processes. Entrepreneur and invited lecturer at the University of Western Australia, Dr Alicia Castillo places the onus on students to come up with a *meaningful* test: does this add value to my life as an individual? Then she goes to the interactions: do I enjoy my clients? The production system? Interactions with my suppliers? etc.. Alicia also adds a component of pleasure and relevance which, through the discussions in class, are noticeable individualistic.

Peter Balan at the University of South Australia gives his classes a single business idea, and then gets the whole class to work on that idea during the lecture/workshop sessions. The challenge is to be creative in evaluating and developing that business idea into a possible venture. Dr Jane Nolan at the University of Cambridge in the UK uses case studies from real life, inspiring people, real life issues and problems which relate to wider society. Students need to be able to evaluate these ideas and understand the opportunities and they work on what makes new ventures viable. In a twist on this process, Dr Elena Rodriguez-Falcon at the University of Sheffield in the UK presents her students with day-to-day problems, such as people with disabilities. This enables her students to use their skills to enhance the lives of others whilst thinking about the commercial implication of their own ideas.

Monica Kreuger of Global Infobrokers in Canada uses several tools to guide this process – and then provides coaching support to help them evaluate what opportunities make the most sense for them given their personal and professional. But perhaps the simplest approach was that undertaken by Dr Caren Weinburg at the Ruppin Academic Center in Israel, who sends her students out to talk to entrepreneurs. Like all things in EE, there is never likely to be a best way to approach such matters. What matters is that you have clearly thought through how you can best help your students to make sense of their ideas and the environment into which they may step. As an EE educator there are several questions that must be contemplated.

## REFLECTING UPON THE UNKNOWN

To what extent do your students remain naïve of the unknown? This is perhaps an impossible question to answer. Let me rephrase it. To what extent do your students become less ignorant of the probable consequences of their possible actions? I have a saying that I display in my office, it says *in the company of my ignorance anything is possible*. I should also display another sign that says *what is possible depends upon who my ignorance keeps for company*. We and our students cannot know the unknown unknowns. We can however spend more time questioning and looking from different perspectives. We can ensure that many new eyes are brought to focus on all the ideas that grace our students' minds; especially when those ideas which relate to a world that our students have little experience of; just like the worlds to be contemplated in the next chapter.

# 9.  Believing and Knowing

The services that ... resources will yield depend on the capacities of the men using them, but the development of the capacities of the men is partly shaped by the resources men deal with. (Penrose, 1959: 78-79)

The physical properties of the materials accessible to man are constants: it is the human agent that changes, his insight and appreciation of what these things can be used for is what develops. (Veblen, 1919: 71)

The two quotes presented above capture perfectly the intended focus of this chapter. As Penrose and Veblen noted many years ago, our capacities to act depend upon our past experiences and current knowledge bases. As EE educators we must understand the intended meaning of these statements. For it is we as educators who frequently are tasked with the challenge of ensuring our students understand the changing nature of the world that surrounds them. It is we the educators who must sometimes hold their hand and guide them towards new knowledge bases and increased confidence.

This chapter therefore seeks to bridge the gap between old style 20th century opportunities and 21st century opportunities and the skills related to observing and exploiting such opportunities. The low-cost of web-enabled entrepreneurial behaviour is discussed from the perspective of how we as educators can facilitate a shift in student confidence. Confidence related to how our students can embrace the raft of low-cost opportunities related to their potential entrepreneurial opportunities.

## ENTREPRENEURSHIP EDUCATION 2.0

In discussing the very exciting technology-based opportunities that are arising for our students in EE, I will do so tempered by the haunting words of Veblen and Penrose presented above. While much is possible it is we that more often than not stand between our students' current disposition and their future development. This creates a potential problem for many EE educators in the world of 2.0. Many educators are not that familiar with how to build a website, how to develop and implement a social media strategy, and therefore how to invite their students into the 2.0 party that is happening right now online 24/7. I have met a few outstanding EE educators who thrive in the world of 2.0, Matthew Draycott in England, Dr Simon Brookes in England, and Associate Professor Geoff Archer at Royal Roads University in Canada are several that stand out. What I observe about these is a general disposition towards the world of 2.0 and a willingness to integrate this into their students learning. Let's take a few moments to consider their various ideas in the world of 2.0; first it's Matthew Draycott, the highly innovative and respected EE educator from England:

> I first began using online technologies as a way of extending the student experience beyond the limitations of my physical classroom. I started with off-the-shelf computer games, using elements of them to help students understand through application how the theory we were learning in class could be utilised in abstract environments and the effects this would cause. Over a period of years I progressed from these early forays into a more systematic use of focused, purpose built simulations at the centre of my teaching practice. Unlike the games I had used before these were true experiential platforms which allowed for a more seamless blend of theory and practice that seemed to better engage the students.
>
> From there I found that I was immersing myself more in the technology and especially how to use multiple platforms to not only create learning environments but to also extend them through the use of virtual platforms and collaborative learning hubs. This means that I could now select tools from a broad range of technological constructs, choosing the ones which I felt were most appropriate to my students and the ways they want to learn in a particular context. Once I understood that I can apply these to create an immersive environment, I then had multiple points of engagement which allows the student much greater freedom in the design of their learning experience.
>
> In terms of my own practice as an educator, my role in the classroom has evolved as a result of my engagement with technology, that's not to say that I have become a back room hermit; creating systems which my students work through, far from it. I am instead an active participant in an evolving learning experience, I am much more a guide through this changing landscape then I am a teacher or lecturer. My role is to help students to interpret the information they find and provide advice when the activities move beyond their abilities. One could debate the implications of this for hours, but for me, I find this deeply liberating as it frees me from a sometimes problematic construct and, I would hope, empowers my learners to become more active participants in their own education.
>
> While I haven't conducted any research on my classes which would support a claim of improved results I can say that most of my students enjoy the experience and are always active in their learning activities, with the majority achieving good grades as a result. Would this be different without the simulations? I cannot say, but I can tell you that I would not be as engaged were it not for the platforms they experience and create, and hope that this is also true for my students.

As today's digital natives enter our classrooms they expect a greater engagement with technology; not just stuffy 'virtual learning environments' used mainly as industry repositories for unread course notes but engaging experiences where technology plays a key role in helping to make learning experiential, not just theoretical and extendable with multiple points of entry and exit to suit the learner. I believe that these systems will be more and more collaborative, expansive and crucially student-centric, moving the role of the lecturer from the wizened soul imparting knowledge from on-high to map maker, guide and collaborator shaping the environments he or she constructs to constantly get the most from the students based on their own activities.

Having observed Matthew's evolution over several years I can attest to his curiosity and constant willingness to challenge his students. It takes courage to attempt to perfect that which is rapidly evolving; that is technology. This is another of the unique learning outcomes I observe for Matthew's students. I see them learning to become adaptable is the spirit of Penrose and Veblen. I see them gaining confidence to contemplate how they might exploit the technological opportunities afforded them. The next example presented comes from a team of educators at the University of Portsmouth in England, they being Sarah Underwood, Simon Brookes and Alex Moseley:

> Giving students the opportunity to act as consultants to a SME within a course is a powerful form of entrepreneurship education. However, there are many practical reasons why this type of education 'through' entrepreneurship may not be feasible; consistency of experience amongst different groups of students, reliability of partner businesses, professionalism of students (not to mention time, resources and staffing). Therefore, the primary motivation for using Pervasive Learning Activities (PLAs) with entrepreneurship students is from a willingness to allow students a similar authentic experience but within the boundaries of classroom-based teaching and without the same resource requirements. PLAs create a richly authentic context for students, blurring reality with fiction by blending simple (and relatively cheap) online technologies (such as websites, twitter, Skype, email) with offline activities more often associated with entrepreneurship pedagogy. PLAs, first described by Brookes and Moseley (2012), are a form of alternate reality gaming whereby the tutor creates a fictitious case study that is augmented by an environment that feels realistic to the students to such an extent that they begin to act as if the experience is real.
>
> In the University of Portsmouth and, subsequently, the University of Leeds, this technique has been used to create both a for-profit and not-for-profit examples of failing businesses set in the fictitious town of Porthampton, UK. As well as both businesses having websites that list a number of personnel that students can *interact* with during their course, Porthampton boasts a city council, a local newspaper and a university website, which provide sources of information to the students (some pertinent to their course, some describing how Porthampton Football Club faired at the weekend).

In both cases, students become part of a training course linked to a Porthampton-based consulting company that provides the primary link between the students and the failing businesses. However, as time goes on, students are expected to collect data for themselves through email and Skype with *staff* from the failing business in addition to more traditional forms of research. Throughout the courses, tutors are acting as facilitators to deliver relevant theories and helping students to develop a critical understanding of entrepreneurship by linking to a *real* experience. Assessments are a mix of company reports, email responses to set questions and reflective essays. More about these examples, plus details of how to build your own PLA can be found at www.pla-academy.co.uk.

The anticipated outcome of these PLAs was that students, having gone through this experience, would have developed entrepreneurship skills as if it was real. Certainly, there was evidence that students had bought into the storyline and the individuals that they had interacted with. Students commented 'feeling as if it really heightened the task significance' and that 'we cared about [members of the business], they mattered to us'. Students also (generally) appeared to want the story to be real, even though they had been told at the beginning of the course this was not the case, commenting 'I remember [the tutor] saying it wasn't real but then I just ... put it out of my mind'. However, this was not a uniform response with a small minority of students unwilling to participate as a role-play character. Despite this, students showed good levels of engagement with the PLA modules and that they had developed a range of entrepreneurship skills, such as creativity, innovation, negotiation, communication and leadership, as a result. In some instances, the fact that the business was not real allowed the students a more unique chance to experiment, as one student commented 'it allowed me greater freedom in terms of innovation, meaning I felt safer in proposing riskier and more radical ideas'.

Having a low-cost yet richly authentic experiences (such as PLAs) available will be increasingly important as entrepreneurship education becomes more deeply embedded into higher education and permeates into more non-business focused disciplines, which appears to be the current trend. PLAs can cut across different disciplines – students could easily delve into the inner workings of Porthampton hospital, local arts group or school. Surely the more meaningful, relevant and fun entrepreneurship education can be made for students, the more they will get out of it?

The obvious benefits outlined above clearly require much planning and commitment. It is no surprise that a team has formed around this project. As educators we frequently have and see great ideas. Sadly, all too often we don't have the time and resources to bring them to our students. Teaming up to share the development and exploitation of such experiences makes sense. I am reminded of the African saying, if you want to go quickly, go alone. If you want to go far, go together. The third example I would like to share with you comes from a very dynamic EE educator, Associate Professor Geoff Archer at Royal Roads University in Canada:

As a result of federal spending cuts, Royal Roads Military College was decommissioned by the Canadian Armed Forces about 20 years ago. Economically inefficient for the military, this large scale change all but abandoned a gorgeous 500+ acre campus replete with laboratories, classrooms, dormitories, an Olympic sized pool, a boathouse, a stone castle and a verdant old growth forest. Fortunately, a prescient group of educators and politicians came together and made a proposal for a new kind of school to be built in this great space. Given well-established local competition for traditional students in a four-year program, Royal Roads University was mandated to be different from the start. The target customer is the working professional, and the education while academically rigorous must also be conveniently accessible. And so it came to be that a Canadian school on an island off the coast of Vancouver came to pioneer the blended learning model-asynchronous, online learning supported by brief on-campus residencies.

Each year more than 500 students take their business degrees from the Faculty of Management. More than 100 of them are studying towards the Bachelor of Commerce in Entrepreneurial Management. This program attracts working professionals in their late twenties to early thirties. The fast pace and team-based pedagogy require that each successful applicant demonstrate a minimum of three years of full-time work experience and two years of college (post-secondary) education.

In the eyes of an entrepreneurship educator the tradeoffs in this system are plain to see. Here are the three most prominent; 1) although working professionals are better at doing startups than inexperienced teenagers they are much less likely to undertake new ventures in real life (given higher opportunity costs, family and work obligations), 2) the vast physical distance between team members increases the diversity of a team's perspective but it also impedes or denies most typical experiential exercises, and 3) keeping all lecture type content asynchronously accessible means that most discussion is occurring in something like M.I.T.'s *flipped* classroom without an actual classroom.

Consequently, my course design and my teaching style have adapted to perform and I dare say excel in this unique environment. I focus on four elements: digestible, concise and compelling reading materials that even the busiest students will still consume, moderated peer-to-peer dialogue that avails the entire class of the lessons gleaned from others' experience, real-world experiential exercises that take advantage of the fact that online students are already halfway to getting out of the classroom, and finally I encourage every student to keep an eye on the practical value or employability of any major deliverable (better a consulting project for an innovative company in a high growth industry sector than a business plan for one teammate's pipe dream).

These *applied* principles of online education have generated dozens of new social ventures in my classes over the past few years. Several of these have carried on beyond graduation, adding value with both double and triple bottom line business models. Famously one exemplar, www.GoVoluntouring.com, was established and sold five months later to the Australian travel giant Flight Centre for what I estimate to be a solid seven figure valuation.

While most of us have invested years or even decades building out our own CVs with training, practice, research and accolades, I believe that the coming changes in higher education, particularly online learning, will require us to re-evaluate our conception of what it means to be an educator. Thinking of ourselves as a *coach* (rather than an orator) is not likely a stretch, as that transition to active learning has thankfully been underway for decades. Being comfortable in our *connector* role, a la Malcolm Gladwell's (2002) *The Tipping Point*, might not come as easily to educators who have been socialised to consider *networking* a distraction from serious work. That said, I believe that an educator's powerful professional contacts might soon tip the scale for a prospective student who is evaluating the cost and structure of a traditional degree versus more flexible and cost-effective formats that are increasingly viable alternatives (e.g. MOOCs). Finally, in a BYOD (bring your own device) era students will benefit far more from learning how to learn than they will from learning anything specific. If knowledge has been so democratised that any literate person with an internet connection can learn how to deliver a baby or start a stubborn lawnmower within minutes, professors need to embrace their *curator* role. Normally a term reserved for museum tour guides, curated has been a hot Silicon Valley buzzword in the years since the ascension of Pinterest, Tumblr and other sites that enable people to gather and display links or images that they find interesting, inspiring or aesthetically pleasing. Considering all it took to attain our influential positions, I imagine some natural resistance to the recasting of our role from Socrates to the DJ of pithy blogs and powerful TED talks. Still, I implore you to consider that the essence of how we add value in the future will likely involve being the person who knows what is worth knowing and where to find it.

I see Geoff as the next generation of EE educator, an entrepreneur making the most of what he can assemble to create immediate value for his students. He is right, the future is upon us and we must ensure we do not withhold our students' access; otherwise they will access it elsewhere. Conversely, I see many other educators who avoid 2.0 technologies at all cost, other than what their institutions require. This makes no sense. If we can agree that entrepreneurship is essentially a process of social change, and that entrepreneurs are therefore agents of social change; then they need the tools of the day to enact it. Today, the name of the game is 2.0, change is happening rapidly and in unpredictable ways. But, the change that is happening is heading in a specific direction; that of an increasing reliance upon technology.

Consider many of the ideas discussed throughout this book so far. What has taken priority in my thinking has been the individuality of each student's approach and motivation to learning. We are rapidly moving away from the use of monolithic technologies such as the educator requiring all students to attend a physical space and progress collectively through the chapters of a specific textbook (Christensen, Johnson and Horn, 2008). Technology is allowing students to customise their learning experience; just as we do as customers in our interactions with the firms we do business with. We are surrounded by this change and our students require from us that which closes the gap between them and such change, and that which enables them to develop confidence in this ever-changing world.

## Examples of Emerging Practice

Charles Wankel (2010) recently published a book on cutting-edge uses of social media in business education. It provides an interesting snapshot of who is doing what. The starting point is that many students are digital natives and thus already have many skills that can be further developed and applied to a business context. While this is true, it loses sight of the increasing numbers of adult learners that are engaging with EE; many of whom have poor skills in this regard.

Putting aside this issue for a moment, we can consider how educators in related areas are using technologies to develop awareness and skills. Most educators use VoIP (such as Skype) to communicate with colleagues and family members, so why not with their students? For adult learners who are tied up at work and have responsibilities to families immediately post work, something as simple as Skype can provide both the educator and students with the means to communicate on learning tasks and/or group projects. Sounds like a simple approach and it is. Increasingly, educators are hosting blogs and other materials externally from their institutions to provide their students with a richer and more meaningful experience.

Clearly there are many lines that can be crossed here between what is an educator's personal time and what is their professional time. This issue I sense is a contributing factor to the low usage of online technologies to teach with. Once we cross this line it is highly likely that to use the technologies effectively other lines become quite blurred. Just as we hold different teaching philosophies, we also hold different views on when one should be available to our students and when one shouldn't be. Personally, I can see the need for consultation times to spill over from the normal 9 to 5 hours. Indicating to our students that they can communicate at certain times after hours will most likely become the norm as we move forward.

One of the emerging possibilities here is to enable our students to help each other through organising and perhaps mediating (and/or assessing) various knowledge sharing spaces. In this way, we do not need to be present while a community of practice develops and takes our place in certain ways. Alternatively, we can be present and guide our students to utilize the internet's connectivity. For example, we can challenge our students to develop a pitch and put it online for comment/feedback. The emergence of crowdfunding requires these very skills, and we need to ensure our students can play in this emerging space. Also, the advent of virtual worlds is reshaping EE. I have come to know Peter Harrington, one of SimVenture's co-founders as a friend, and I am forever amazed at his energy and passion to reshape what it means to learn about business experientially:

> When I was first invited as a guest speaker to talk with business and entrepreneurship students about my experience of creating and running companies, I was introduced as a course *highlight*. Whilst my billing came as quite a surprise, I was keen to make my time with the group of 80+ students worthwhile. As such, rather than just talk at the seated audience I focused on two hands-on, and what I hoped would be engaging, activities. Fortunately for all of us, the afternoon passed without major incident. No one nodded off or walked out and a genuine sense of *uplift* ran through me at the close.
>
> Over the next couple of years I was asked to repeat my guest-speaking role on different occasions and as such, I spent time in several academic environments. But almost by osmosis I discovered the quality, speed and accuracy of subject learning was often adversely affected by the educator's lack of practical experience and more significantly the dearth of appropriate and inspiring educational resources. For me, the resource problem became most evident when I was asked to be a judge on a university business planning competition. This event was supposedly the course showcase. However, nothing in the demeanour of the students (who presented their *original* plans to an audience of 7 judges), nor the quality or appropriateness of their hypothetical thinking, gave me any real confidence that this somewhat artificial approach to learning added real value.
>
> My experience in academia fuelled wider market research, which sought to establish how nascent entrepreneurs learnt and how they were being taught and trained. The findings ran consistent with what I found before; as a result a small team gathered, considered the issues and within 4 years SimVenture, a business simulation that allows people to create and run a virtual small company at no risk, was launched. The formative research with students, teachers and budding entrepreneurs demonstrated that the traditional, often didactic approach to EE was not that effective. More importantly, the research uncovered 3 fundamental principles that we felt should underpin high quality EE resources:
>
> • Experiential resources that engage minds typically lead to entrepreneurship students being more likely to want to learn and thus care about their work.
>
> • Resources need to be as authentic as possible so that learning is put in real-world context where people can apply thinking meaningfully and recognise the longer-term value of their work.
>
> • Resources need to be sustainable and flexible. Educators are often time poor and curriculum restrained. By allowing them to become facilitators

of student work they can maximise teaching efforts and operate more efficiently and effectively.

Back in 2006 when we launched, a simulation seemed an obvious fit with EE; it used appropriate technology, promoted personalised (as well as team) learning and required students to act and respond experientially rather than be passive receivers of information. At the same time, a simulation provided an opportunity for user decisions and corresponding data to be captured thus creating powerful content for post simulation reflection and presentations.

Today SimVenture is used in over 40 countries and provides a clear business context for both teachers and students. The resource helps educators to understand how a micro as well as small business functions and students are able to develop their own mental model and thus experience how the different business disciplines fit together (rather than learn in subject silos). To make SimVenture as authentic as possible nothing is left to chance when the simulation runs. Students must manage money, look after their time, develop skills and keep an eye on tiredness and stress levels. Even though there are multiple difficulty levels, the algorithms have all been written so students must think their way through all the related challenges presented within the game – rather than hoping they get lucky. SimVenture is designed to inspire learning and develop critical thinking. Given the fact that every economy around the world needs better business start-up and survival rates, it's imperative that we give people the best opportunities to practice and fail as much as possible before starting or running a business for real.

I believe entrepreneurs such as Peter Harrington and innovations like SimVenture will become increasingly common in our world. They are so well developed and offer so much value to students that this is inevitable. The challenge for EE educators will potentially be both increased and decreased by such innovations; the question for you is how and to what extent?

## THE PROMISE OF NEW WORLDS

The advent of the plethora of online platforms available to educators will radically change our approach to EE. When we take stock of the transformation that has occurred globally over the past 20 years, is it any surprise? Simply having experience running our own start-ups will no longer set us apart from the run of the mill business school educator. We need to lead the way, collaborating with others to gain access to new knowledge so as to ensure our students' learning is current and engaging. We need to use platforms like SimVenture to provide our students with access to that which we have not the expertise in.

I sense a real state of excitement at present, dare I say, an entrepreneurial spirit in the air. The practice of the EE educator is increasingly spilling over into the world that lies beyond their actual students. Content is being created for one purpose and being shared for other purposes. Educators are spending less time creating resources and more time directing their students towards someone else's resources. This mobility while breathtaking also potentially looms as a threat. If we cannot create sufficient value ourselves in the learning activities that come before and after such mobile content, the roles we play in our students' education may be lessened.

I truly believe that the majority of EE educators I have had the pleasure of knowing demonstrate an innate curiosity to explore the application of such technologies. I sense we are an innovative lot who grow restless repeating anyone particular learning activity for too long.

## REFLECTING ON MY PRACTICE

In terms of my personal approach to using technology, I would admit to being a bit of an addict. However, rather than building platforms to deliver a curriculum, I seek to turn the technology over to my students' imaginations. My favourite exercise is an activity I call the value creation challenge. It provides students (in small groups) an opportunity to develop a website and also a unique value proposition. In addition to this, they must also develop/execute/monitor and adapt a social media strategy for their website. This task has been deliberately designed to challenge my students. In the absence of any formal instruction beyond a workshop related to building a website and the strategic use of social media to attract visitors to a website, they must find a way to succeed. The students can make a website based upon any issue (other than something related to pornography, violence etc.). I encourage the students to create a website related to world events occurring during the evaluation period. Typically, they focus upon sporting mishaps, humours or something tourism oriented. Their task is to develop content that will hold the interest of the visitors they seek to attract to their website.

I observe that most students use social media strictly in a social manner blissfully ignorant of its strategic application. So while they find navigating around such tools easy enough, they need to be led towards an appreciation of how to use tools such as Facebook, Twitter, LinkedIn. They demonstrate amazement when shown how even email can be used in a strategically targeted manner. Once the students have created their website, prepared their social media strategy, I introduce the assessment of the challenge. This usually occurs over a ten to fourteen day period. Pivotal to the students learning is a daily statistics report sent to each group that enables them to gauge their performance and attempt to maintain/remedy their performance.

This challenge enables me to address a range of difficult to 'teach' aspects of the students' learning. It allows them to learn skills that have a high value in today's increasingly online economy. Skills that typically need to be developed through the experience of doing, rather than listening, skills that once developed can be reapplied elsewhere with ease. I also sense that EE provides too little attention to the mental health challenges associated with being an entrepreneur. Students breeze into and out of our classrooms, free to direct their attention elsewhere. As educators, we know that in reality entrepreneurs have no such luxury, their dreams and adventures torment them for better or worse, 24/7. This challenge ties the students' success to their ability to organize themselves around a *live* challenge ensuring little room to hide the lazy, distracted or simply missing in action student.

There is a hard cold reality to the students' progress through this challenge. They are assessed across a range of metrics, including their organisation, their measured performance and their candour of their self-evaluation. While the students are excused for failing, they are not for covering up their failings. This challenges typically provides students with a confronting experiences in which their assumptions are sorely tested against the reality of the foreign world they temporally are required to step into. However, my confidence in the challenge increases every time I use it. My students grow in leaps in bounds, proudly presenting me their individual assignments and/or community based interventions via their newly minted websites that they have personally created. Without doubt one of the best gifts we can bestow upon our students is to provide them with the independence to navigate the world of 2.0.

## SUMMARY

> The continuing mission: to explore strange new worlds, to seek out new life forms and new civilizations, to boldly go where no man has gone before. (Star Trek)

I wish you well on your journey into the unknown. I am frequently reminded of the red queen principle (Van Valen, 1973), which asserts that in an ever-evolving system, individual continuous improvement is needed in order to remain competitive relative to the system you are co-evolving with. In the spirit of this observation I wish you well in your quest to explore strange worlds, seeking out strange new technologies and to use them in innovative ways that add vale to your students' development.

# 10. Ideas and Business Plans

No business plan survives first contact with customers. (Blank and Dorf, 2012: 35)

In contemporary EE there is perhaps no more controversial topic of debate than the business plan. I will not attempt to hide my own personal biases; I see very little reason to ask an entire class to each write a business plan. As always, it is you the reader who must determine your position on this issue. Rest assured I will not be blindly cheering on the alternative lean start-up (Ries, 2011) or customer development methodology (Blank and Dorf, 2012). I also see problems in the implementation of these ideas in EE as well. I also will not be arguing the case for effectual logic (Sarasvathy, 2008). Perhaps it seems there is little left to discuss? I think not. The arguments I will present in this chapter I contend address a common problems present in most of these increasingly popular approaches; that of naïve and/or lazy assumptions.

This chapter considers the evaluation of our students' ideas, of assisting them to step out and embrace the reality of their markets, communities and end-users. Building upon the sense-making framework discussed in chapter 8, the aim is to present a non-prescriptive framework for enabling our students to act and then plan rather than planning to act. The key issue of *study time* is accounted for in this regard with consideration given to the priorities of their educational outcomes. Let's briefly consider the nature of the debates that surround the issue of the business plan.

## THE BUSINESS PLAN

Within Academia, the business plan frequently dominates EE, commonly seen as a mechanism of risk management through which both internal and external benefits can be derived (Barringer, 2009). Externally, potential investors are provided with an overview of the entrepreneur's opportunity and the plans to pursue it. Internally, a road map has been created to help keep the entrepreneur on track. When these two perspectives are united, there would appear a simple logic as to why any entrepreneur would write a business plan before engaging in the process of starting-up a new business.

As supported by Hisrich, Peters and Shepherd (2010), the road map analogy has significant traction in academia; if we plan to go somewhere, we improve our chances of getting there. However, beyond the confines of academia, the business plan would seem to be increasingly losing its standing.

Many have resorted to taunting the business plan as a work of pure fiction, a document about an opportunity that is rarely understood in it's full detail prior to the plan being written, and thus quite likely to lead anyone in the wrong direction (see Mullins and Komisar, 2009). Others argue that it is an over-complication of process, that young nascent entrepreneurs should simply be encouraged to try things first and just see what happens (Guillebeau, 2012). Others suggest we as educators must ensure we remove overconfidence or hubris (Kaufman, 2012) from the plans our inexperienced students create.

## REASONS WHY NOT TO WRITE

However, the actual nature of our students' required learning is too often left out of this debate. It seems that the debate is tethered by the opinions of academics that believe or don't believe. We owe our students much more than to simply fall back on personal opinions. Recent research by Jones and Penaluna (2013) presents eight arguments why writing business plans are an inefficient use of time for the majority of EE students.

### Unproven Performance Links

Despite the logical claim that prior planning should increase eventual performance, there is little empirical evidence that this is so. Lange et al., (2007) argue that in the absence of any need to raise serious capital, there is no need to write a plan. Thinking that is supported by Bjerke (2007) who contends that the unpredictable nature of entrepreneurship renders the process of such planning obsolete. Bill Bygrave (2010), with reference to a quote attributed to Winston Churchill noted 'However elegant the strategy, you should occasionally look at the results'. The suggestion being that if we substitute *business plan* for *strategy*, the quotation hints at the dilemma faced by proponents of business plans. The work of Lange et al., also provides little evidence that directly relates the skills of writing a business plan to actual superior performance or start-ups and/or firms in general. Indeed, to draw further on Churchill's observations, a distinction is made between setting plans and developing the capacity to innovate and outwit for competitive advantage (Rankin, 2008, p. 37). I contend, the latter should be more the focus of EE than the former.

## Reality of Start-up Funding Needs

The assumption that students of EE should carry around a business plan in their back pocket and lurk in elevators hoping to strike the jackpot by bumping into a venture capitalist is mere myth. Ask yourself this question; how many of *your* students have been funded by a venture capitalist immediately after or during your guidance? Assuming the answer is less than 1%, we need to ensure that we focus on what is most likely to happen in the lives of *our* students, not what might happen elsewhere. The business plan is predicated upon the process of start-up and the subsequent need to obtain substantial funding. In reality, the vast majority of start-ups (for better or worse) commence without any such funding (Shane, 2008). Shane advocates that we should not oversell the 'entrepreneurship via start-ups' pathway to all and sundry. Indeed, to the extent that we are working with valid and well thought through assumptions, we will have most likely bypassed many of the demands for significant capital funding. The reality is that an entrepreneur's resource profile counts for more than their vivid imagination nearly every time.

## Assumption that our Students always have Great Ideas

Asking students to focus their attention on developing an idea and then writing a business plan assumes something very important. It assumes they are capable of creating great ideas at will. While it may be countered that getting students to write a plan will help them to test their ideas, why not just let them do that first? A logical question would seem to be, are we putting the cart before the horse when we start with documentation/evaluation strategies, rather than generation strategies? As a result, our students tend to gravitate towards many similar types of ideas year after year. This seems to suggest a form of mediocre idea generation to me. Surely given the obvious diversity of our student cohorts from one year to another they should be bringing forward new and innovative ideas. What we seem to get are the ideas that are suited to writing a business for.

## Type of Thinking Encouraged by the Business Planning Process

Returning to the notion of brain plasticity, we need to again ask, what type of thinking are we trying to develop/encourage? Jones and Penaluna (2013) note that research into cognitive neurology highlights the fact that normative assessment strategies limit the students' propensity for new and challenging thought patterns. Given that it is desirable to challenge our students beyond their existing mental endowments in ways that motivate them, writing a business plan does not really fit the bill. In fact, what we need our students engaged in is the excitement of communicating new ideas and pitching scenarios rather than documenting assumed factual realities. This may seem harsh. I accept that many EE educators are brilliant at assisting their students to write well written business plans, but few will be the by-product of the type of thinking we would generally aspire to create in our graduates.

**Actual Life Trajectory of our Students**

From where do your students come? To where are they headed? Can you honestly see a business plan being used somewhere during this journey? I think that for the less than 10% of my students who want to create some new vale and will need to be supported by external investment, they should have a business plan. However, such experience and knowledge need not come at the expense of the other 90% of students who will not rely upon the presence of such a plan. In my personal situation, I provide other resources that allow me to impart guidance on the development of a business plan. During this process I work as a mentor to those students who are in need of such assistance. However, it is the needs of the many that outweigh the needs of the few. My position in this regard is not borne from my attitude to business plans, but rather the limited space in the curriculum and the pressing need to include other matters.

**New Approaches to Planning**

If business plans fail upon first contact with the assumed customers (Blank and Dorf), perhaps we should ban customers so that our students can complete their work in peace. Seriously though, I support the notion of naïve business plans containing faulty assumptions. The notion of developing the customer and product simultaneously as espoused by Blank and Dorf and Ries (2011) makes more than sense than not doing so. They bring the focus onto the plan's building blocks, that is, the untested assumptions within.

Gone is the opportunity for students to make blind leaps of faith and to bury untested assumptions in their work. Students are comfortable to do this for they already realise the highest hurdle they face is their educator's judgment, good bad or otherwise. The obvious disconnect between the reality of what is contemplated and what is assumed is all too evident when reading a student written business plan. We do our students a disservice when we allow their assumptions to be merely judged rather than actually tested.

While the customer development and lean start-up approaches are to be congratulated for getting our students out of the classroom and out face-to-face with that upon which they speculate, there is still a potential flaw in the approach. We can't assume that the assumed customers will be customers and we can't assume they actually know what needs to be known. We also can't assume that the assumptions developed are the most important assumptions vis-à-vis the actual eventual process of selection acting for or against. So while I am supportive of this approach, I urge caution against rushing the process of developing assumptions and assuming specific areas of risk. In reality, the sense-making framework in chapter eight will most likely lead to a raft of additional and potentially more important assumptions than most other ways of evaluating ideas. The reason for this is that is based upon what happens in reality, rather than what insightful and wishful thinking can conceive.

## Advent of the Effectuation Phenomena

Much has been made of the emergence of effectual logic (Sarasvathy, 2008) in the domain of EE. Read et al (2011: 7) see effectuation as 'using a set of evolving means to achieve new and different goals. Effectuation evokes creative and transformative tactics. Effectual logic is the name given to heuristics used by expert entrepreneurs in new venture creation'. Are you concerned by this statement? I certainly am. It would seem that the starting point is the expert entrepreneur. I worry about a theory built around the cognitive abilities of experts with regards its application to novices. As educators, we are not even working with seasoned or novice entrepreneurs. To be frank, quite often we are not even working with nascent entrepreneurs. Putting this concern to one side, let us move further into the world of effectuation to consider its use when writing a business plans.

Read et al. (2011) see the business plan as a marketing tool, a mechanism for communicating to a desired audience the nature of the objectives determined to be related to the development of new value. Encouragingly, they suggest it should bring about a sharper focus to the nature of risk, rather than too optimistically developing the upside of a given idea. So focusing upon likely bottlenecks and posing *why* questions to find ways of overcoming any such problems. This sounds like an improvement of the more linear traditional business plan. It would seem in this context students are required to think more laterally in search of solutions to possible problems.

The plan is seen as a necessary evil given that investors and/or the ever-present business plan competition require such objects. Read et al. (2011: 154) state that there is a 'difference between a causal business plan and the effectual business plan ... that in the effectual case, it is not a plan – it is merely a communication tool written over and over again as the venture develops and [is] written differently for different stakeholders. Honesty demands that effectuators do their best in building predictive models but explicitly clarify that the aim is not to deliver on the plan but to do what it may take to co-create value for everyone involved'. At this point I have walked away from the process. A document that is continuously rewritten by expert entrepreneurs as the actual new venture unfolds against the reality of its time. There would seem to be a very clear mix-match between the underlying philosophy of the effectual business plan and the reality of the typical postgraduate student. For this reason, I see this approach as also too heavily relying upon assumptions that are most likely false. Although in this case, the assumptions are less about the idea and more about the writer.

## Requirement to Develop Flexibility Rather than Single Plans

What is it we are trying to develop in our students when they write a business plan? Many definitions of entrepreneurship include creativity and/or innovation, yet in a business plan context, the assessment of such abilities appears to remain problematic and largely ignored. As Pittaway and Edwards (2012: 293-4) conclude, 'there is a need for further research that explores assessment practice in entrepreneurship education in disciplines outside of business schools … [where] … other forms of entrepreneurship education, assessment practice tends to be more reflective, more engaging of other stakeholders, more accepting of ambiguity and more formative in nature'. Many educators grade the plan depending upon how well they see it executed and/or how they assess the viability of the proposed business.

With the business plan as the focal teaching and learning tool, our learners are typically encouraged towards finding a singular linear solution, rather than considering a whole range of potential solutions, which may in turn, better inform an approach that accommodates ambiguity, shift and change (Jones and Penaluna, 2013). I have always liked an approach that goes along these lines. Student presents his or her idea, states the capital requirements to get the ball rolling. The idea is evaluated vis-à-vis the validity of assumptions related to resource profile, customers, marketplace and technologies. Assuming the idea has merit, the student is sent away with the task of trying to figure out how it could happen without any such assumed capital funding. It is amazing what students can conjure up if given a few alternative pathways to travel.

In summary, across the eight issues briefly discussed, many challenges to the traditional and non-traditional business plan have been considered. I would argue that the primary limitation of the traditional business plan is that it typically need only survive in the rarefied air of the educators' judgment. In terms of educating students this simply isn't good enough. Such an approach doesn't present a sufficient challenge or offer avenues towards building motivation. It is merely a task that requires completion. There are many educators who see an important role for the business plan in our students' education, and many whose approach is mediated by the context of their teaching.

## REASONS TO ACT AND/OR PLAN

'The business plan, although often criticized as being dreams of glory, is probably the single most important document to the entrepreneur at start-up stage' (Hisrich, Peters and Shepherd, 2010: 187). In the United States, it has previously been stated (Honig, 2004), that 78 of the top 100 Universities favoured the business plan. Assuming the second claim to be true, clearly the underlying assumption here is that the student of EE is going to at some point in their life start a new business. So, to be fair, let's hold that assumption as being a reasonable one; let's assume that our students most likely will start a new business.

Bridge and Hegarty (2012) provide a first-rate overview of the use of business plans in higher education. They observe that business plans are expected to play a uniting role, capturing all the essential elements of the curriculum. This is a perspective widely shared in the literature. This is consistent with Stevenson et al. (1999) who argue that a business plan is a document that articulates the critical aspects, basic assumptions and financial projections regarding a business venture. It is also the basic document used to generate interest and attract support, financial or otherwise, for a new business concept. Put simply, 'it is what you intend to do, where you intend to do it, how you intend to do it, what resources (internal and external to you) will be required to do it, and what degree of sustainability and performance is expected' (Jones, 2011: 126-127). Again, the primary assumption being that the student wishes to start a business.

Given that we know that the majority of students of EE do not at present start a business, we need another reason to favour its inclusion in our curriculums. Well, it seems eminently sensible to plan for your success. Especially when there is no doubt that lending agencies and various types of investors demand a business plan to evaluate any such investment opportunity. Previously, I have noted the process perspective as an argument supporting business plans Jones (2011: 127). Typical of the responses reported was that 'understanding the business planning *process* is a critical skill and tends to help students understand how to gather pertinent data and present it in a convincing manner'. Further, that 'learning to modify developing concepts based on evolving data are important skills to being an entrepreneur and/or an intrapreneur'. In a similar vein, 'the *process* of developing a business plan (if properly taught and managed) is a great learning tool regardless of whether the concept comes to fruition'.

Pleasingly, I sense that the tide is turning; that various blended approaches are in fact emerging that accommodate both sides of the debate. This I believe is evidenced by the responses contained within the IE-II Survey. Educators were asked about the importance they placed on getting their postgraduates to first go out and meet their assumed customer prior to actually beginning the planning phase, versus writing a plan and then presenting a product or service to the assumed customer. Monica Kreuger of Global Infobrokers in Canada requires her students to talk to the proposed customers first to open their eyes and guide their future decisions. She argues a business plan is a plan of decisions and they need first-hand information as part of the research bank. Although she saw the need to get the ideas down on paper before they talk to customers, but felt decisions could not be made without the latter.

Dr Jane Nolan at the University of Cambridge in the UK felt that no customers or market equals no business opportunity. Jane gets her students to think about unmet needs, potential customers, markets, market sizes and dynamics. Are these real needs, which will be sustained? If not, Jane saw no point in doing the business plan. In a similar vein, Peter Balan at the University of South Australia has as his standard and first requirement in postgraduate courses an assignment requiring an interview with an entrepreneur. Each student is also required to carry out face-to-face interviews with target customers. Peter insists that a plan without such documented evidence from target customers does not have much value.

Context is clearly also important as not all EE happens in the business school. Annette Naudin at Birmingham City University in the UK opts for the acting first approach, but even that has some level of planning. Annette's students do not write business plans. Basically, it is always a balance between presenting and planning ideas and testing the idea with their network, potential customers etc. Annette ensures an emphasis on having a go rather than desk-based research. Context also matters to Dr Elena Rodriguez-Falcon at the University of Sheffield in the UK. Elena works with engineering students, a field which implicitly encourages you to meet the customer first in order to assess their needs (market research) and then develop the solutions to their problems (engineering), before commercialising the product (business planning and marketing).

Of course there are many other ways in which the business plan is used as a learning process. Associate Professor Elena Pereverzeva at the Moscow International Business School in Russia uses the process in a dynamic manner. During the course Elena's students develop a business plan and implementation plan. After they finish the course they have access to business plans competitions and the opportunity to present the outcomes to potential customers. Alternatively, others see the business plan as a process that accompanies other learning outcomes. Dr Bill Kirkley at Massey University in New Zealand encourages a *proof of concept* approach to valorisation, which is to validate and realise. Speed to market is emphasised, and the process of business planning goes on in the background and is used primarily as a means of achieving further investment. Likewise, Assistant Professor Eric Liguori at the California State University in the United States focuses on action in all his courses, planning is typically second, as Eric uses action to gain access to proof of concept.

## REASONS TO THINK ABOUT BUSINESS PLANS

It makes sense to understand the various positions our colleagues adopt and/or develop regarding the use and/or adaption of the business planning process. My position as stated in chapter eight is that making sense of the environment of a business opportunity and therefore the nature of possible strategies to exploit the idea come first. Only once a student is confident they actually know what types of selection are operating can or should they consider writing a plan or engaging other alternative approaches.

This is where I sense my approach is different. The easiest thing our students can do is develop a long list of assumptions they hold regarding their idea. However, in reality, they are wasting their time and ours if the assumptions are not even remotely germane to the processes of selection ultimately working for or against the idea. While it is possible for the entrepreneur to change aspects of his or her selective and ecological environment, this should never be taken for granted.

Which brings us full circle back to where the chapter started, I contend a common problem at present in most approaches; that of naïve and/or lazy assumptions. I think we as educators have a duty of care to ensure that what we set out to teach can be learnt. We need to ensure that not too many abstract ideas are used throughout the process. We need to ensure that our students can learn and demonstrate their learning in their here and now (Whitehead, 1929).

Given the acknowledged differences our students present with, in terms of knowledge, experience, motivation and aspirations, we must tread carefully here. There is however a way in which each student can have their knowledge and experience fully employed whilst also increasing their motivation vis-à-vis their general aspirations. To conclude this chapter we must return to the ideas central to the development of the reasonable adventurer. The type of undergraduate student I seek to assist in the creation of. The attributes of which I maintain in conjunction with the attributes of self-authorship contribute to the development of the tethered adventurer.

## AN UNCOMMON INTEREST IN THE COMMONPLACE

> The new, the bizarre, and the strange beckon us all. What separates the Reasonable Adventurer from us is his [or her] uncommon interest in the commonplace. Somehow in the ordinary more is seen, more is felt. (Heath, 1964: 34)

In this wonderful observation above is a hidden gem of wisdom; one that we have the opportunity to take advantage of. Assumptions that our students can conceive ideas about which to write a business plan ignore the reality of their actual lives. They require of the educator ability to gift wisdom and understanding that most likely does not exist. In all truthfulness, I come across very few students writing business plans about something they have lived, breathed and experienced; they tend to write plans about that to which they have possibly desired, but rarely experienced. In Figure 10.1 the logic of my thinking will be introduced.

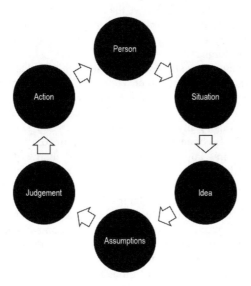

*Figure 10.1   The circle of situated knowing*

My students are people; they have imaginations that are fallible; they have energy that is already committed to the future; and they're knowledgeable about a great many things that others are not. When I read a business plan, I am reminded of these truisms. My students cannot know the future and/or how their ideas may perform in a future world. They arrive before me with a raft of pre-existing commitments that are largely binding and not negotiable. However, when we as educators step into the wonders of their individual worlds we mostly find that they are experts about something that occurs in *their* world.

This I contend *must* be the starting point for the students' thinking, regardless of any continuity that they perceive between their current and future worlds. If we as educators do not understand the world of the student, the gap between their imagination and the reality that exists in their world we encourage fantasy. If we do not understand their capacities to contribute beyond their pre-existing commitments we encourage day dreaming. If we do not understand what they know and to what they are capable, we deny them greatness. Everything else counts for little. Whether they write a plan or not matters even less.

Figure 10.1 illustrates a logic that runs along these lines. A *person* cannot be transformed into something they are not. They are a product of their *situation*. The *ideas* they pursue should therefore be born from the experiences they have had in their situated lives. To the extent that this occurs, the *assumptions* they make about what they know and what they are capable of will more likely be ground in reality. Their closeness to such reality can increase the probability that the *judgements* they make in evaluating their idea will be reliable. Thus, any *action* undertaken to pursue their idea will have been done so relying upon what can be known and what they are capable of doing.

The extent to which they should be governed by other factors as well, will be discussed in the following chapter. However, in summary it is important as an educator of EE that you neither blindly reject or accept the business plan and associated planning. My preferred choice is to allow my students to evaluate their ideas using my sense-making framework. Done properly they will typically find less than they hoped, and quite often, more than they assumed. I see in my approach the infusion of many of the alternative approaches alluded to in this chapter. The difference I sense is that my students will solve their problems in this regard through choosing the bits and pieces that suit the circumstances of their life.

In closing, take the time to reflect upon the pathways you introduce your students to. Are they required to take directions to a known destination, or do you let them to wander freely in the identified reality of their own life? We will surely differ in our approach here, which is fine, so long as we also allow our students to differ in their approach too. To paraphrase Heath (1964: 35), I see all of my students as having a deep understanding of knowledge not necessarily because they are more intelligent, but because they have been there.

# 11. Connecting for Action

The desire of gold is not for gold ... it is for the means of freedom and benefit.
(Emerson, 1904: 234)

What is it our students seek and what is it we as educators give? As an educator in the world of EE, I experience many moments of guilt, of uncertainty about my influence over the experiences shared between my students in the learning environment we co-create. I worry that I have deprived them of a raft of traditional theories that others place great importance on. I worry that I have left them to dwell on who they are and how they relate to the process of social change. I ask myself repeatedly; do my personal experiences as an entrepreneur influence their opportunities as learners more than they should? I ask why have so few of my postgraduate students have entered the fray of entrepreneurial bedlam? What would compel them to do so post their interaction with their EE experience? My experiences tell me that there are many paths our students could tread; yet there are only a few that they should (or could) travel.

## A PATH WITH A HEART

In this chapter I am seeking to share with you as educators the most intimate of moments I share with my students. I am inviting you into the world where my moments of guilt invariably are overwhelmed by the reality of my students' lives. I am sharing with you that which keeps me my path with a heart. The moments in time that flowed to produce what you will soon read were designed to be highly provocative. I hope for you the same level of reflection as you walk the same cognitive pathway my students walked. The practice I will now share with you followed the group sense making process discussed in chapter five.

The process beings with the presentation of a situation statement, in this instance an excerpt of Carlos Castaneda's (1968: 81) *path with a heart*, I share this reading with my students at the completion of the course, and it seems appropriate to do so with you as we draw towards the end of this book.

What follows then is the presentation of the situation statement as experienced by my students and their contributions to the four stages of the group sense making process. These reflections relate to their intentions to pursue the idea they walked through the sense-making framework discussed in chapter eight, and/or, other possibilities they observe in the world they live in.

## Situation Statement

*I was recently given Carlos Castaneda's The Path with a Heart to read (reproduced below). What struck me is that when I'm happiest (and most energetic) I'm travelling a path with a heart, and when I'm not, I seem to be directed down some other sort of path to (generally) satisfy someone else's dreams. How about you?*

Anything is one of a million paths. Therefore you must always keep in mind that a path is only a path; if you feel you should not follow it, you must not stay with it under any conditions. To have such clarity you must lead a disciplined life. Only then will you know that any path is only a path, and there is no affront, to oneself or to others, in dropping it if that is what your heart tells you to do. But your decision to keep on the path or to leave it must be free of fear or ambition.

I warn you. Look at every path closely and deliberately. Try it as many times as you think necessary. Then ask yourself, and yourself alone, one question. This question is one that only a very old person asks. My benefactor told me about it once when I was young and my blood was too vigorous for me to understand it. Now I do understand it. I will tell you what it is: Does this path have a heart? All paths are the same: they lead nowhere. There are paths going through the bush, or into the bush. In my own life I could say I have traversed long, long paths, but I am not anywhere. My benefactor's question has meaning now. Does this path have a heart? If it does, the path is good; if it doesn't, it is of no use.

Both paths lead nowhere; but one has a heart, the other doesn't. One makes for a joyful journey; as long as you follow it, you are one with it. The other will make you curse your life. One makes you strong; the other weakens you. The trouble is nobody asks the question; and when a person finally realises that they have taken a path without a heart, the path is ready to kill them. At that point very few people can stop to deliberate, and leave the path. A path without a heart is never enjoyable. You have to work hard even to take it. On the other hand, a path with heart is easy; it does not make you work at liking it. For me there is only the travelling on paths that have heart, on any path that may have heart. There I travel, and the only worthwhile challenge is to traverse its full length. And there I travel—looking, looking, breathlessly.

*So what about you and your idea? How about you and your current trajectory in life and/or your capacity to contribute positively to some aspect of economic/social development in your area? Are you on a path with a heart?*

The comments below are as my students made them, they are linked as indicated across the four phases. As I read these comments my mind returns to the nature of the issues canvassed in the first three chapters. These issues play out in the lives of our students in the most personal of ways. We cannot influence their composition within our classrooms, we cannot assume control over them, but we can observe and understand them. That is the aim of this chapter; to invite you into the minds and hearts of my students. Let's start with my students' *feelings* toward the situation statement.

## Phase 1 Comments

Reading the statement made me FEEL vindicated that the path I am currently on is a path with a heart. I have travelled many paths in my own lifetime and many have led nowhere. There came a time in my life when I reflected upon the path that I was on, I was fortunate to walk a different path that I could choose to take. The statement confirmed my feelings which I too FELT; that if the paths without a heart were chosen then they would probably end up killing me. I FEEL sadness for other people who may be on a path without a heart, but circumstances may not allow them to be able to choose a path with a heart that may lead to happiness. The current path that I am on is one of discovery and challenge, there may be obstacles that I need to overcome in the future, but I am smiling and travelling a wonderful path. (student comment no. 1)

After reading the statement I FELT that I could easily apply this to my own life. I am on a path that financially I cannot get off. I FEEL that this statement is similar to the saying that if you are paid for doing something you love, you will never have to work a day in your life. It has the same meaning in that if you enjoy what you do it doesn't really feel like work. I am FEELING stronger about finding something that I am passionate about and will try harder to make this happen. Forget about the financial restrictions and just go for it. I FEAR this could also be a selfish path to take as it would impact upon my family and the comfortable life they live which is associated with the path that I am on. Unfortunately many do not have the option to take a path with heart and are forced work hard to stay on their current path, hoping that in the long run it will all pay off. (student comment no. 2)

The situation statement made me FEEL reassured and at ease at my current stage in life. The whole concept of everyone having a potential path of heart, and the ability, regardless of its difficulty, in changing to it is extremely positive. On both a personal and professional level I believe I am on a true path of heart. I am not only happy with my character development, relations and friends, but the profession that all these aspects have assisted me in venturing into. I FEEL fortunate to be in both a profession and community that I can provide social and economic assistance. However after reflecting on some of my close friends, and their current paths, I FELT disheartened knowing that several of them hadn't found theirs, and consequently not achieved a similar level of peace and satisfaction. Should I assist them in finding it? Or would I be adding bias towards my path of heart? (student comment no. 3)

I FEEL that I am too young and my blood is too vigorous to really agree with the statement. I FEEL that the statement is stifling – why should I not choose the ambitious path? Perhaps ambition, learning and achievement are where my heart lies; I have certainly enjoyed my path through this life so far. I FEEL that the statement may be beyond my experience – I have never followed a path through life so far because others willed it, it has always been my choice. (student comment no. 4)

I FEEL lucky to have stumbled onto the pathway of working with people with disabilities to find employment. It not only energises me but challenges me at the same time. Nothing gives me more of a buzz than to see someone achieve and do something they really enjoy and to increase opportunities in other areas of their lives – we often take for granted. I spent many years working to earn a living not really enjoying the work and it showed. My passion came from working with people and the sense of achievement and the FEELING I had made a small difference. It became even closer to my heart when two of my immediate family members were impacted by their disability and the challenges to find and maintain employment. Now I am older and somewhat wiser I now understand to be happy and fulfilled there has to be passion. (student comment no. 5)

I FEEL that we all have our dreams and set our own paths but the truth is that we have to let our FEELINGS take us down other paths to allow us to get to the dream. If we let how we FEEL keep us on a single path we will probably end up going around in circles and getting nowhere. I FEEL that it's like a tree we can go many ways but to reach the top we must be prepared to hit dead ends and wrong turns to get the FEELING of satisfaction that we have reached the destination of our dreams. (student comment no. 6)

Wow, this is so true. I have always thought that the greatest sin is to have a wasted life, to reach the end and find that you ignored your heart and spent a lifetime pleasing others, being trapped when you weren't, or following falsehoods. I spent all of my 20s doing that, working in a job that I hated, that ensured poverty for my family and myself (and not just materially). I dreaded each working day, trapped in a working life that was a dead end and that made no difference to people lives. I knew that I had to make a choice that would be difficult and may have led to nothing. I knew I needed to do it for me and my family. What a liberating and rewarding choice it was. To be able to liberate my mind, to build something from an empty sheet of paper, to make a difference to others and also to me and to meet some fantastic people. What rollicking fun. What a challenge. (student comment no. 7)

Reading the situation statement for the first time caused me to be overcome with a very strong FEELING and sense of awareness. As I read over it the second and third time I found this shifted to a deep FEELING of responsibility. It really reiterated that the only thing keeping us on the path we are currently on, be it good or bad, is ourselves. As I thought about the statement further, the feelings it triggered within me personally and the feelings it caused others in the group to experience I started to feel extremely grateful, sad and empathetic. I understand that my mind and my actions, which I am fortunate enough to have complete control over will move me towards or away from a path with a heart. I am also aware and FEEL saddened by the reality that some people, through no fault of their own, are not so lucky and do not have the faculties we all too often take for granted to literally take control of their lives by getting on a path with a heart. (student comment no. 8)

When I read the second situation statement I FELT that I could relate to following a path with a heart and understood the meaning. I FEEL agreement that traveling a path which follows the heart is much easier than following a path that a person may not agree with. However I FEEL that to follow a path only by heart is very difficult, yet I agree that at least asking yourself if you are following a path which has heart is right. I FEEL that a path that may not have heart could lead to a path that does, I ask myself; is this one path or two? (student comment no. 9)

When I initially read Situation statement 2; I FELT SUSPICIOUS, I FELT like there must be more to this seemingly simplistic approach to the journey of life and the paths we chose to follow. Then it struck me 'To have such clarity you must lead a disciplined life'. I FELT relieved! It is simple and yet at the same time complex, I FELT. I FEEL we must be patient, self-disciplined and very self-aware in order to choose and tread a path of the heart in CONTRAST to that of a path I FEEL *is expected* (by our environment) for us to follow. I FEEL that whilst it is true that self-discipline is something that we as a culture accept is infinitely easier with age, I FEEL I must challenge that notion. I FEEL that as children we possess this quality and that society forces us to accept that we MUST travel and accept paths with no heart, in order to be accepted as normal. I FEEL as older people we learn to be accepting of ourselves and listen to our heart, I FEEL we gain self-appreciation, acceptance and discipline by realising that we FEEL the urgency of being true to ourselves as we realise our own mortality. We FEEL we want to *make a difference* and FEEL urgency to leave behind a positive legacy. I FEEL this in turn leads us to FEEL self-discipline, FEEL focus and gain perception. I FEEL my idea is one on the path of the heart as is my life in general. You see, I FEEL my heart beat faster and my vision clearer: when FEEL conscious of my legacy which I FEEL is my children's future/community. (student comment no. 10)

After reading the situation statement I reflected upon my own life and the paths I have taken. I FEEL that I have always made conscious decisions to work toward my life goals, thereby creating the heart of my life path. I concur with the statement that I too FEEL greater happiness, energy and satisfaction when my path has heart. My presentation reflects a path with heart – my ideal situation which will enable me to assist others to find their own path with heart plus providing me with an opportunity to grow across so many areas of my life. Unfortunately I FEEL that the heart within my current path is waning as I have become impatient and even disheartened by my current limbo state. Time is needed for the situation to resolve so I need to create the heart so that this period passes quickly. (student comment no. 11)

I FEEL that when you a truly on a path that is heart-warming to you your path will flourish and produce far greater results than if you're traveling a path that your heart is simply not in. I FEEL that people can and do take different paths in life the heart path and the going through the motions path, but the heart path is truly the results path. I FEEL that although the challenges I face with my idea and my current pathway, my heart is truly involved in the direction I am taking. (student comment no. 12)

Reading this statement I FEEL accepting of the message it conveys that a person should be true to themselves and follow their own path in life, while many paths exist not all paths will have a 'heart' that is to say not all paths will encompass a 'passion' which can be sought or in most cases found. While everyone will always be on a path, even if they have passed along a path, they may not share a passion for that path. It is important to be mindful of what you truly enjoy and pursue your dreams. Much like the situational statement this piece is about awareness of self and having hopes or aspirations that people can find their own path in life that they can take the journey of the heart to wherever that may lead them. (student comment no. 13)

When I read through this statement it made me FEEL proud to be working in the area that I am passionate about and truly enjoy and am interested in. I FEEL honoured to be surrounded by people who clearly are either already on their paths, or starting to make their way towards a life of passion. I FEEL this passion and journey of the heart are essential to succeeding, and will ensure that we all pick ourselves up again and push on even if we do fail along the way. (student comment no. 14)

This statement sings to me – I feel so delighted to read it. Workwise I am taking a circuitous route along a path that has MEANING to me; I have jumped off the path when it has made me unhappy. I am glad to read the thoughts of someone who can articulate what I FEEL about life, work and following ones dream. I am surprised at the bit about leading a 'disciplined' life as I have always FELT that this way of thinking is the complete opposite. (student comment no. 15)

The situation statement made me FEEL inspired and comforted as it suggests that we all have choices and should not be held hostage to pathways, which affront our personal values and goals. Furthermore it encourages us as individuals to take control, make decisions and it gives permission to withdraw from circumstances that suppress or limit our desired outcomes. However it made me FEEL concerned that not all people in our society have the same opportunities and choices to pursue their dreams; it simplifies the challenges that many individuals face in our community. Society is iniquitous and isolates individuals who may not have the social, economic or spiritual means to choose an alternative path. For example how can one who suffers the monotonous cycle of illiteracy or the isolation of living with a disability, simply choose another pathway and follow their heart. The irony in this statement is that it may be a privileged few from society who are truly free to pursue their pathways unencumbered of duty and responsibility. Finally, it made me FEEL challenged that to change pathways one must be courageous and be prepared regardless of their own personal shackles such as mortgage, debt and dependency to make a leap into the unknown to pursue their pathway with a heart. I FEEL unsure as to whether I am following a pathway with a heart, or am I a victim of society's expectations and shackled by the burden of responsibility and commitment? (student comment no. 16)

I FEEL a sense of happiness to read this statement because it so clearly encapsulates why I do the work that I do and also why I am so happy within my work. My work is my passion and my passion is my work. This statement also allows me go some way in answering why some people around me are not content or within their lives. It may be because they are not on their path living their dream or following their heart. This makes me FEEL even prouder and more satisfied that I am living my dream and so comfortable with my path and passion and that I'm following my heart. (student comment no. 17)

I feel spoilt that I can find myself continually in the middle of such diverse feeling. It is the reward I receive for employing such powerful tools of reflection. However, at this point in time the process of reflection has only occurred between the student and myself. Moving on to the next phase reveals the extent to which each student understands the challenge of connecting to and staying on a path with a heart.

## Phase 2 Comments

Having read the other students feelings, it was apparent that most of us were on some sort of path with a heart, whether it be at work or with life in general. I FELT that I agreed with the comments that the path with a heart may come later in life, when we can be truly responsible for the actions on which we choose to take. It also appeared that students who did not think that they were travelling a path with a heart were searching for that particular path. THIS MEANS were very similar with this statement, which I FELT was open to interpretation of our FEELINGS and understanding of entrepreneurship. (student comment no. 18)

Having read through the responses I have an over whelming feeling of jealousy towards others who are on a path which has heart and feeds their passion. I am now feeling even more empowered to choose the correct path for me. The feeling I am getting from others is that we would all like to be on a path which has heart for fulfilment in our own lives but it is not always possible at certain times in our life. I THINK THIS MEANS there are times in our lives when we do have the ability to choose the right path for us which has heart and generally I am feeling that people do take this path when the time is right. (student comment no. 19)

When I COMPARE and CONTRAST my feelings with our class I noticed a general consensus on the overall message taken from the situation statement. The comfort gained from knowing you are on a path of heart was shared by all. Unlike the previous statement, there was little division within the group in regards to feelings and thoughts throughout the statement. It was more focused on what sections related more too each individual. It is worth noting that depending on each person's experiences, there were mixed responses with regards to the difficulty in changing, and more so finding, one's path of heart. I BELIEVE THIS MEANS that such a diverse group, all coming from different walks of life, is bound to have mixed emotions and thoughts in regards to the finding and changing of paths. I think this also emphasises the fact that the stated level of clarity needed to look outside of your current path is difficult to achieve, and that the whole statement follows an easier said than done approach. (student comment no. 20)

COMPARING the responses to the 2$^{nd}$ situational statement offered me some food for thought. The comments about some not having the choice or resources to follow the pathway of the heart really drove it home how lucky I am to have a choice and the resources to change if needed. In CONTRAST I didn't acknowledge that following your heart or being passionate is not totally exclusive to my working life. WHAT THIS MEANS FOR ME – I could not be truly happy in my life if I was part of something where I FELT uninspired or disengaged. Thankfully, I am inspired by people everyday, whether it be family, co-workers or people in my community. (student comment no. 21)

After COMPARING my classmates' statements I have noticed that there is a lot of heart involved, and lots of being overwhelmed. In CONTRAST I feel that I did not think deep enough and after reading through others statements there is heart and lots of being overwhelmed involved in any path we take in life. I THINK THIS MEANS I now realise that I act way to fast before actually thinking. (student comment no. 22)

That was interesting! I read the postings and a couple really hit home for me. The point was made about the difficulty of just changing if you don't have the resources to do so. Perhaps we need to experience those difficult tasks in a significant way before we can understand what our heart truly wants. But I also loved the comment about the statement singing because that's what it does for me. As was said, to be with people that have truly chosen to follow their heart is wonderful, not some new age fad of the moment experience but to have truly followed your heart. A life well lived must be the ultimate accolade at a funeral. (student comment no. 23)

After reading the postings made by the rest of the class I believe the situation statement and what it is suggesting has been widely accepted. I THINK THIS

MEANS that one way or another each of us are able to relate a previous experience or a particular period in our lives to the message we interpret it to be giving. This could mean that naturally we subconsciously apply the message/meaning to the particular area of our life that is predominantly important to us. I think this broader acceptance of each other's thoughts, feelings and beliefs along with societies at large could very well mean this course has actually begun to expand our minds and further open our hearts. (student comment no. 24)

After reading the phase 1 group sense of my fellow classmates I can COMPARE how I FEEL and how most of the class FEEL that following your heart is the best path. In CONTRAST to some of the class who appear to be already travelling on a path with heart I FEEL my own path is still progressing to a path with heart. I BELIEVE THIS MEANS I am travelling in the right direction. (student comment no. 25)

I FEEL that feelings COMPARED to most; we collectively seem to FEEL that in our earlier years and/or at certain times of our lives we are almost always forced into a position of soldiering on, on a path with no heart, in order to FEEL normal, make a crust and consequently avoid poverty. I feel that some of us by CONTRAST some have not discussed how they FELT about the notion that one must be disciplined to take a path of the heart. I think THIS MEANS that that though we gather as a class of a diverse age groups we are all interested in entrepreneurship and innovation by and large, we aware of our *path with heart,* and most acknowledge that this these path/s is the route to a worthwhile and fulfilling life, and that the *discipline* required may be *discounted* by the burning desire to live a life with heart. (student comment no. 26)

Upon reflecting on my own feelings in phase one and COMPARING them to and CONTRASTING with those opinions of the class, I feel that the responses across the class could be described as *heart felt.* Most reflected on their own lives and the paths that were followed, some through necessity others because of responsibility to others. Some described paths as requiring discipline; others considered the privilege of choice; some described the need for courage; others felt the one path leads to another. I THINK THIS MEANS that while most reflect upon their own life experience that provided them a choice to choose their life path – many accept that there are others in the community who do not have this opportunity. Therefore, creating a life path with heart, should be considered a privilege, as many, due to their social position, do not have the life choices that we experience. I feel that effect of this statement could be described as the stone dropping in the pond, I hope as we all return to our own life paths the ripple effect will continue and we all become more conscious of supporting others to create and follow their own path with a heart. (student comment no. 27)

When I look at the other student's postings, I THINK THIS MEANS, that there was broad agreement of the sentiments expressed in the passage. However I found it interesting that most students compared it to their workplace and occupation rather than their entire lives. I think that this is consistent with society's preoccupation with occupation. We determine a person's intelligence, success, happiness and well-being simply by the job that they do. These views are full of contradictions and biases and are entirely misleading. I believe the pathway to happiness is not solely about employment but a number of deeper considerations and that an individual must consider all of the pathways collectively to determine whether they are truly happy. (student comment no. 28)

Having read my classmates' responses to the statement I FEEL there was an overwhelming acceptance for the statement. Many people found the passage to be comforting to them and also to be reflective of their current path. I FELT surprised however that there was no contradiction to the message given the motherhood nature of the statement. In some responses to the statement I also FELT a sense of obligation to follow your heart causing some class members to FEEL a level of responsibility to their cause or a responsibility to find one. (student comment no. 29)

At this point in time, my excitement rises as I see my students become aware of how those around feel and understand the situation. It is all well and good to assume that our students can become entrepreneurs, but ultimately life always comes first, or worse still, gets in the way. I think this aspect of the students' thinking is best captured in a few of the comments from the next phase where they're thinking collides with that of a chosen person who is external to the class.

## Phase 3 Comments

After showing this statement to my partner and one of her friends I got a response of what the %$#&, I now realise what we have learnt in class. This VALIDATES to me that I am not the only one who can easily be confused. After explaining some of what we had discussed in class, they started to understand. But from they're initial response, this VALIDATES that if we think to quickly we will be led down the wrong path and we will not fully understand what the statement is trying to tell us. (student comment no. 30)

Like many here I chose my partner when seeking someone to read the situation statement. The text resonated with her as she's not long left a job to pursue a career in something she loves, starting her own business. She noted her joy at being able to follow something that has been her passion over her previous 9-5 job that dominated her life until then. She did however note that following your path also causes stress of a different kind. What if you fail, what if it's not what you want, what if it ends up costing you financially. Dreams are all very well, but they can become nightmares if not built around a disciplined set of actions. (student comment no. 31)

My friend read the second situational statement. She agreed you can only have a choice to follow your own heart path if you have the resources available to afford choice. She FELT the decision about whether to stay on the path or leave it due to fear or ambition was very true – nothing holds us back like ourselves and our circumstances. She did VALIDATE my stated position regarding my choice to leave a job where I was unhappy and agreed a path without heart is never enjoyable. She FELT I was one of the lucky ones where my pathway found me. She said it would be difficult for her to make a change to follow her true heart path due to the constraints of her family, mortgage and lifestyle commitments. Her FEELINGS were based on fear of the unknown and the risk of personal failure. (student comment no. 32)

I showed the statement to to my sister. She VALIDATED my own response to this statement and said 'that is all very well, if you do not have to pay rent'. We both agreed that a path of the heart is an ideal way to live, where you create a career and life out of doing what you enjoy and value. Both of us felt that the idea of work has changed in that people no longer focus on survival but want to combine this with having a purpose. (student comment no. 33)

When I shared this statement with a friend, the response they gave me was that they had worked hard their whole life to find the path they are currently on, and that they could not be happier with where they are in life. This does not VALIDATE my view on the matter, though I must ask myself if my friend really considered other people in different situations than her own when making her response. Like me, she has had the means to follow her heart from the beginning. (student comment no. 34)

After reading the situation statement my partner commented that she thought everyone would want or wish to follow their hearts in all they do regarding their career path and in life but unfortunately for some it is not a realistic option. It's great to dream for some and even strive to that goal but some simply cannot get there. Reflecting on the response my original opinion was VALIDATED by the fact that most people gravitate to a life or career close to their hearts however I understand it is not always possible. I feel that people would somewhere along their life paths have somewhat of an opportunity to walk a path close to their hearts, some take the opportunity some don't, some seek the opportunity early in their live and some leave it until later in their lives. (student comment no. 35)

I showed the statement to my husband. He thought about it for a while and said he thought a path with a heart (for him) is loving what you are doing. He questioned planning goals – are they something to highlight a path or just a distraction from a path? He thought all paths lead nowhere inferring life is about the journey, not the destination. We talked about it and did wonder if it is difficult to have the clarity of vision to see the path with a heart at times. It is not black and white – the path may have a bit of a heart and you may not be totally happy but you can't see anything any better at the time. I was glad to hear what he had to say as we have discussions on and off over 25 years about this subject, in some form or other. He once said I was fanciful in wanting employment that was what I considered socially responsible. He may still think this but accepts the importance of being happy in what you do (however that occurs). I like his comment about the journey being more important than the destination – this supports my thoughts. His comments VALIDATE my thoughts and support my approach to the path I have taken. (student comment no. 36)

Now I can see to what extent my students see themselves as agents of change. To what extent they see themselves as someone capable of stepping into another role in society. I can also see to what extent they are already on a path with a heart. Knowing this is critically important to the relationship I develop with each individual student. Knowing a student is heavily committed to the demands of their current life, but nevertheless already travelling a path heart enables me to focus on the specific aspects of their life to within which they could become more entrepreneurial.

## WORKING WITH WHAT MATTERS

What matters to us matters less than what matters to our students. We can easily overstate the importance of a variety of issues in EE. When all is said and done, our students' passions and therefore their motivations already lie deep in their hearts. I believe our effectiveness as educators is increased when we managed to get inside the hearts and minds of each student. Then we are able to help each student contextualise the learning opportunities EE makes possible. Dr Jane Nolan at the University of Cambridge in the UK captures this nicely I feel, noting that students will have greater awareness as a result of their enterprise education which may mean they may well take an idea forward at some time. However they may do so as intrapreneurs. Their entrepreneurialism may enable them to be more innovative in their drive to change their world, even if they don't start a business.

So, how do you approach this with your students? Are you comfortable with the permission your students have to dream? Are they able to contemplate how their learning relates directly to their life and the challenges they face daily? To assist our students connect for action we need to understand where the action is. We need to enter that world and tease out the nature of the assumptions they hold. We need to provide them with feedback not on what they know relative to a specific knowledge base, but rather with regards how they see such ideas as being applicable to their lived life.

The final chapter now awaits; presenting you with an opportunity to revisit your thinking vis-à-vis the ideas discussed thus far. I invite you to become a critic of these ideas. I invite you to become a critic of yourself. But most of all, I invite you to consider your students as reluctant entrepreneurs, but potential entrepreneurs nevertheless. I dare you to rise to the challenges scattered throughout the final chapter; become the educator your students deserve!

PART IV

Creating Community Leaders

# 12. You are Not Alone

Start where you are, use what you have, do what you can. (Arthur Ash)

You are you and can be no one else. You owe it to your students to be you; authentic and of value. Throughout this book I have asked you to reflect upon many issues I feel of importance to the development our postgraduate students. In this final chapter I wish for you to contemplate the challenges and future challenges we as entrepreneurship educators will most likely face. Unlike the mist that shrouds our undergraduates from the immediate reality of their future, our postgraduate students arrive seemingly simultaneously ensconced in their past, present and foreseeable future. Many seek assistance and knowledge that has a very short shelf life. Our ability to mentor their development is paramount and we need to be either very talented or very socially connected to satisfy their needs. You can do no more than start where you are, use what you have, and with some luck and persistence, do what you can to assist your students' development.

This chapter aims to revisit my personal observations of the challenges we face teaching postgraduates, as discussed throughout this book. It is important to appreciate that every educator's practice is not developed overnight, but rather through trial and error processes occurring over many years. You are entitled to be less than perfect in the development of your approach.

## TEACHING WHO YOU ARE

Our starting point in this journey was the nature of our teaching philosophies. Knowing who you are relative to the process of EE and your students' aspirations is fundamental to you being an effective educator. From my personal experience and through conversations this process of self-knowing cannot be rushed. Just as we become wise over time in other aspects of our lives, so we do as educators. You can help yourself by developing an enquiring mind, asking questions continuously. I have been influenced by many great minds and it was through my natural curiosity that I found their potential contributions to my practice. How much time do you spend talking to colleagues? How many other EE educators have you contacted to seek advice and ideas from? I find that collectively we are a very generous bunch of educators, always happy to assist others to explore their practice.

If we met, would I sense the *fever* for learning you use to infect your students with? Be that your passionate disposition or your control of the facts under your control. I sense a wonderful opportunity for us all to develop pedagogical content knowledge of EE. To raise the bar of scholarship related to our practice beyond that of our fellow educators in closely related fields. In doing so we could work collectively, supporting each other's practice and setting standards for those who follow behind us. We also have the opportunity to separate our respective approaches to working with undergraduates and postgraduates. This is critically important, as hopefully the many ideas addressed through this book demonstrate.

I invite you to contribute to the development of pedagogical content knowledge in our field. In doing so I dare you to delve deeper into your soul, to find that which truly directs you to appear before your students at your best. Collectively we can move our field forward and ensure its longevity. We can celebrate our diversity of approach and gain a deeper appreciation of the contextual challenges we all face. I believe our collective futures will be greatly enhanced through our advancing this opportunity.

## ANDRAGOGY TRUMPS PEDAGOGY

To many the adult learner is a threat, a student of potentially superior standing. Perhaps they are already an entrepreneur, perhaps they have achieved much professionally, or perhaps they are just simply incredibly curious. I can honestly say that I have never felt inferior in the company of my students and/or colleagues. This is due to the fact that I do not see myself as the holder of all the knowledge and wisdom they would seek. I see myself as merely the facilitator of their learning journey. A journey within which they must find their own motivations; a journey that has no obvious end point or pathway for that matter. A journey that will however be travelled with the experience and wisdom accumulated through the trials and tribulations of adult life.

Here lies the most important difference between the undergraduate and postgraduate contexts. We must adapt our practice to cope with and serve the learner who arrives before us *in situ* vis-à-vis their life's journey. A fixed curriculum while possibly germane to a few students will be hopelessly irrelevant to the majority. Our skill is allowing the manifestation of our students' motivations to the direct the requirements of their knowledge bases.

In doing so we become less important as the central figure in the classes learning experience. It is within the richness of each student's life that we can operate in ways that maximise their levels of motivation.

As I previously suggested, consider a series of lines whose intersection represents a point in time. Consider those lines as representing our students' awareness, confidence, motivation and sense of stability. As educators, we can place ourselves at those intersections; we can replace darkness with lightness, fear with confidence, ignorance with awareness and instability with stability. But we cannot place every student on the same intersection; for their different life journeys have been travelled on different roads. They each have an intersection that represents their personal histories. Our job is not to simply help them create a roadmap. Rather, our purpose is to enable them to understand the roads they have travelled, the wisdom they have collected along the way, and to help them understand how they can move forward to be the best possible community leader they need and/or agent of change.

## FOCUSSING UPON TRANSFORMATION

At the start of chapter 3 the lizards that adorn the front cover were considered by way of analogy. I wonder if you have subsequently contemplated the nature of that reasoning since? My aim was to challenge you to consider the potential power that reside in your abilities as chief architect of an environment designed to aid transformational learning. Can you envisage your students moving from one context where their recognition of opportunities is less than what it could be, on towards a context in which their abilities in this regard have advanced significantly?

Are you up to the challenge of transforming your students? Are you willing to understand the individuality of your students so that you can challenge them in ways that challenge each and every one of them? Engineering a degree of difficulty beyond that of the students' current abilities, whilst also ensuring that the challenge presented occurs in parallel to an appropriate motivational state. Lastly, are you committed to ensuring that appropriate forms of feedback guide the students' development? Rising to this challenge will most likely deliver *benefits* to the student. To the extent that genuine excitement can be garnered within our students to learn how to solve problems or take advantage of opportunities in their lives, the structural brakes that reduce plasticity over one's life can be relaxed.

This is our purpose, our sole reason for being in the lives of our students. We must *teach* them something *about* entrepreneurship. But we must surely enable them to *learn* more *for* and *through* entrepreneurship. Importantly, we need to allow each student to commence from their own starting point and finish where they deem appropriate.

## TOWARDS YOUR IDEAL GRADUATE

I have identified two types graduates, the reasonable adventurer and the tethered adventurer. The primary difference between these two types of graduates is when and where they might create value. I see the reasonable adventurer creating most of their value in a time and place associated with their future. Alternatively, I see the tethered adventurer creating most of their value in a time and place associated with the life they are already situated in.

Accepting the responsibility of being a transformational educator comes with a price. That price is knowing *how* to create a particular *type* of graduate. While the reasonable adventure is built around the development of six specific attributes (Jones, 2011), developing the tethered adventurer requires that I reshape 'what they believe (epistemology), their sense of self (intrapersonal), and their relationships with others (Interpersonal)' (Meszaros, 2007: 11). Knowing in advance the nature of the challenge that confronts gives me a chance of succeeding; certainly more chance than succeeding at creating a graduate I cannot imagine.

So the big question, what type of graduate are you seeking to create? Maybe you have a few types in mind. I see my role as creating a meta-graduate, someone capable of operating successfully within different contexts. Perhaps your students are more managers than they are community change agents. Perhaps they are more full-time students, yet to be bashed and bruised by life? It matters little, just step back and dream of what your perfect graduate might be able to achieve. Once you know what they should be capable of you can work backwards and reverse engineer the process required to develop them.

## WORKING WITH ALL THE INGREDIENTS

My most anticipated moment at the start of each semester is that moment when the students introduce themselves to each other. I enjoy seeing their personalities take their first steps, some displaying extreme humility while others seemingly boast of their incredible achievements. In between, the pragmatic folk find the middle ground more comfortable. At this moment, I am excited; all the ingredients have been laid before me. I start contemplating what discussion topics will help me to draw upon their respective wisdom. I am freewheeling just feeding off their responses and trying to observe the extent to which I can draw them together.

Collectively my students will always know more than me, to think otherwise would be ignore their diverse and wonderful talents. My skill is to use their knowledge as if it were my own, to draw from them what I do not know, what my students need to know. One of the ways I am able to do this is to use the process of group sense making. This process allows me to walk through the minds of each student with every other student not far behind me, metaphorically speaking.

How much effort do you make to get everything out of your students that can be used to develop them? I once read that in the 1930s if you had a PhD you were considered an expert on practically everything. However, by the 1980s if you had a PhD you were considered to be less ignorant of one particular aspect of society. I see a lot of sense in this idea. If you do too, what might this mean for your approach to using your students' wisdom? Putting aside the fact your students may not have too many PhDs, they are likely to collectively know the intimate workings of more industries than you. They are the most unique resource in the room; use them.

## BEYOND THE INKWELLS

When I was young child of about seven years old I returned to my school from the long summer holidays. I remember going into a different building and being given my own desk with a hinged table top that opened to reveal a secret hiding place for my books, pens and pencils. I thought this was pretty cool. I noticed something strange about my new desk; it had two holes on the front edge. I wondered what might be the purpose of these two holes. I soon found out that the holes once accommodated pots of ink so that past students could write with a quill pen. I could imagine such implements, yet I found it hard to comprehend how education operated without ballpoint pens.

Roll forward 40 years and I still feel a similar sense of disconnect when educators describe the learning environments they share with their students. All too often their learning environments have walls, doors, data projectors and whiteboards. I struggle to confine my students' learning to such a place. To do so is to admit defeat. It would be to say that when my students assemble at a time and place of my choosing, this corresponds with their learning. It would mean to say that what happens outside of this place is not really learning, because it was not included in the initial description of the learning environment.

When we tie ourselves to forms of experiential education processes we need to do so with uncommon vigour. We need to release ownership of the learning environment, inviting ourselves into the worlds our students occupy. My fascination with the work of Beard and Wilson (2002) has really helped me to understand where I need to travel to be present in the learning moments my students experience. I understand my role in developing the outer world of the learner. I understand how I need to be mindful of the sensory interface of the learner. Finally, I appreciate and seek access to the inner world of the learner. When you consider the boundaries of your students' learning environments, do you consider the *places* where learning occurs? Do you ask what will our learners actually be *doing* when learning? Have you developed an interest in how they will *experience* their learning? Are you able to account for the nature of the *emotional* engagement related to their learning? Have you fully considered what our learners need to *know*, and finally, have you determined how our learners can be encouraged to *change*?

The world is rapidly changing; technology is turning the traditional learning environment on its head. The inkwells may remain, but they will never be used for their original purpose. The landscape is open for enterprising educators to stand up and find innovative new ways to work with their students. Stay close to your students, it is far easier to build an extended learning environment around the nature of their lives than it is to try and get them to adapt to our best guess.

## MIND THE GAP

It is easy to fall into the trap of assuming that the resource profile our students present with will be significantly improved upon that of our undergraduate students. The idea that our postgraduate students should automatically present with better resource profiles ignores the fact that any resource profile is idea dependent. Yes, our students have had more time to develop meaningful social relations and industry experience. Yet they also frequently develop social and human capital that may be quite unrelated to the idea to which they are most passionate. There is a need to demonstrate the implications of any such gap between a student's vision and their resource profile. Once there is adequate realisation of the actual landscape that is imagined vis-à-vis the student's resource profile, the true nature of the landscape starts to emerge.

# BUILDING AND DESTROYING ASSUMPTIONS

The greatest gift your students will ever give you will be a glimpse of their dreams. The responsibility that comes with this gift is enormous. Overstate their likelihood of success and we risk causing them future pain, understate the potential value of the idea and we risk introducing future anxiety. While we cannot know the future in advance, we surely can move our students closer to their future, hopefully providing them with a clearer view of what may lay ahead. The environmental interaction framework that I have introduced aims to do just this. I want to lay bare the assumptions my students create to a reality that is difficult to see. I want to help my students create many more assumptions that may move them towards or away from committing to their idea.

My experience with this framework is that it captures both the darkness that hides in unforeseen corners and also shines additional sunlight onto the dullest of ideas. The greatest challenge my students face is in conceptualizing the dimensions of the environment they will interact with and most likely alter. Introducing them to the idea of the selective and ecological environments provides the required clarity for their judgment to become stronger.

Once students can see the process of change occurring naturally around them in and around the area they plan to act, they become cautious optimists, perhaps better described as possiblists. The processes of value creation emerges as do the nature of stakeholder interactions. If they are to proceed, they seem more capable of eliminating many avoidable mistakes. However, without doubt my greatest contribution to their thinking is assisting them to see the emergy related to their idea.

Understanding what assistance is freely available contributes to one's planning in ways that overcome limited resources and other normal constraints. The greatest gift you can give your students is to remove a significant degree of their naivety. I am sure you can devise an effective approach to assist your students. I the absence of such an approach, please feel free to try the environmental interaction framework as outlined.

# LEADING THE WAY

The world of 2.0 is upon us all, it is impacting every aspect of our lives. Your students depend upon you to lead the way. Use it or lose them; that is the reality we face. Don't allow yourself to be swayed by the luddites that warn you about your lost time and constant headaches attempting to tame the beast that is technology. Human history is the story of never-ending technological evolution. We find ourselves in a period of time when the rate of change has never been so sustained or as fast. You have two choices; play the game or get left behind.

The examples of innovative practice I have shared with you demonstrate that we can invent and reach for off-the-shelf solutions. Regardless of your approach, ensure you know why you need to use technology before you choose any type of technology. Doing it the other way around is like setting an animal trap from within the inside of the trap. Consult your students, colleagues and partner with others already one step ahead. Most of all have fun and seek out ways to use the interactivity afforded to you in the world of 2.0 to make your life and that of your students easier than it was before you engaged your suite of technologies.

## PLANNING TO ACT

We are spoilt for choice in how to assist our students' plan for their immediate futures. Truth be know, they already know how to act, their mere presence in your company demonstrates that. However, defaulting to the business plan as an appropriate means of planning for the future is all too often the standard approach for EE students. I have not attempted to hide my biases surrounding this issue. I wholeheartedly believe your students should act upon the assumptions and plan when required after first having acted.

Yes, my notion of *acting* does not extend to actually starting a business. I am referring to the process of developing assumptions in a rigorous manner. Being able to foresee the unforeseen and test both intuition and emergent knowledge is critical. To have written a business plan before having explored every assumption contained within is akin to jumping into a swimming pool without knowing how deep that water is. Perhaps you are a devotee of the business plan? If so, it makes sense to think about how you can incorporate into the process the opportunity for your students to test what they will ultimately write. Ultimately, consider the gift you intend to provide your students, and be guided and motivated by this intended gift.

## THE PATH WITH A HEART

Over the course of a child's life they will receive many gifts from their parents. Some will be cherished and never forgotten, others hardly noticed and forgotten in no time at all. What a pity, I am sure the parents' hearts were in the right place. However, this matters little in comparison to the child's heart. The same is true for our students; we can give our students something from our hearts and yet see them left with little. What matters is what's in the heart of every student.

Never lose sight that their motivation and willingness to take up your challenges will be directly related to how much heart they have to give to your challenges; especially once they step outside your classroom. Let them bring their heart along for the ride; don't be afraid of the student whose heart does not rise to the occasion. Respect their hearts and they will respect you too.

## THE END OF THE ROAD

I feel that I have now travelled up and down both sides of the same road. However, I feel relieved we have travelled this far without any consideration of what should comprise your curriculum. For this surely means that our students' development has remained our central focus throughout. I will sign off with one last piece of wisdom from John Ruskin (1917: 194) whose words remain no less provocative and insightful today than when first written:

> The question as to what should be the material of education, becomes singularly simplified. It might be matter of dispute what processes have the greatest effect in developing intellect; but it can hardly be disputed what facts it is most advisable that a man entering into life should accurately know. I believe, in brief, that he ought to know three things:
>
> > First. Where he is.
> > Secondly. Where he is going.
> > Thirdly. What he had best do, under those circumstances.

I wish you well in your quest to support your students understand their circumstances.

# Appendices

## APPENDIX 1: INTERNATIONAL EDUCATORS SURVEY II

From January 2012 to March 2012 an online survey was distributed to educators known to the author and others holding membership at the online entrepreneurship education portal, www.entrepreneurshipandeducation.com. In total, 51 responses from 20 countries were received. The breakdown of the response was as follows: Australia (8 responses), Canada (1), Chile (1), Costa Rica (1), England (12), Germany (1), Ireland (2), Italy (1), Macedonia (1), New Zealand (1), Nigeria (1), Norway (1), Oman (1), Portugal (1), Russia (1), Scotland (1), Thailand (1), Turkey (1), United States (9) and Wales (2).

### General Characteristics of the Respondents

With regards to teaching experience, 82.4% of the respondents taught at both undergraduate and postgraduates level. The majority of the respondents had been teaching entrepreneurship for more than five years (51.0%), with 21.6% having more than three years' experience but less than five years' experience, and only 7.8% less than three years' experience.

The vast majority of the respondents (74.5%) were classed as full-time academics. In terms of start-up experience, 53.9% have been or still operating their own business. In terms of the most common approaches to teaching entrepreneurship to postgraduates, 88.2% felt their students learnt from each other, 74.5% used high-level experiential learning activities, 60.8% claimed to use reflective practices with their students, and 56.9% stated they arranged for their students to work closing with practicing entrepreneurs.

# APPENDIX 2: EXAMPLE SITUATION STATEMENT

As I drove back to Hobart on Saturday afternoon, I reflected on the possible trajectories of the students in BAA517, vis-à-vis their future capacity for enterprising behaviour. I thought that sometimes we (i.e. society) place too much emphasis on the presence of the heroic entrepreneur, a person capable of moving mountains. That this approach can defeat the ambitions of the meek in a moment's thought.

Alternatively, I thought that the notion of an uncommon interest in the commonplace has much merit, because when we can conceptualise entrepreneurial behaviour as being related to upsetting the status quo then it could be related to the simplest aspects of society.

*Figure A2.1    Ever-present student diversity*

What is always present is diversity within the student group. When I look at a classroom of students, as illustrated in Figure A.2.1, I see varied levels of commitment, or ambition, of talent, of curiosity, just as it should be. For if the entire world was occupied by entrepreneurs there would be insufficient structure to enable sustainable growth and productivity. Perhaps what I was seeing in my mind looked like the illustration below.

We meet students when they encounter a 'classroom experience', some have been entrepreneurial in their lives, and some have not within the context of the heroic notion of the 'entrepreneur'. We suggest they could proceed to live an entrepreneurial life in the context of a dynamic worker, a servant to social causes and their community, a saviour to those seeking to exit self-employment or a creator of a new enterprise. But should we also create a pathway for an honourable retreat. A pathway for those that are naturally drawn to protecting the 'status quo' to exit the process? A place to which they could return somewhat wiser to the nature of the entrepreneur and their propensity to change the world they live in.

# References

Aldrich, Howard E. (1999), *Organizations Evolving*, London: Sage.

Aldrich, Howard E. and Martha A. Martinez (2001), 'Many are called, but few are chosen: An evolutionary perspective for the study of entrepreneurship', *Entrepreneurship: Theory and Practice*, **25** (4), 41–57.

Amburgey, Terry, Tina Dacin and Dawn Kelly (1994), 'Disruptive selection and population segmentation: Interpopulation competition as a segregation process', in Baum, Joel A. C. and Jitendra V. Singh (eds), *Evolutionary Dynamics of Organizations*, New York: Oxford University Press.

Aronsson, Magnus (2004), 'Education matters – but does entrepreneurship education?', *Academy of Management Learning & Education*, **3** (3), 289–92.

Ash, Arthur, 'BrainyQuote', http://www.brainyquote.com/quotes/authors/a/arthur_ashe.html, (accessed 10 October 2013).

Baldwin, James (1896), 'A new factor in evolution', *American Naturalist*, **30**, 441-451.

Bain, Ken (2004), *What the Best College Teachers Do*, Cambridge, MA: Harvard University Press.

Barringer, Bruce R. (2009), *Preparing Effective Business Plans: An Entrepreneurial Approach*, London: Pearson Education.

Bavelier, Daphne, D. M. Levi, R. W. Li, Y. Dan and T. K. Hensch (2010), 'Removing brakes on adult brain plasticity: From molecular to behavioral interventions', *Journal of Neuroscience*, **30** (45), 14964-71.

Baxter-Magolda, Marcia (2004), *Making Their Own Way*, Virginia: Stylus.

Baxter-Magolda, Marcia (2007), 'Self-authorship: The foundation for twenty-first-century education', *New Directions for Teaching and Learning*, **109**, 69-83.

Baxter-Magolda, Marcia (2008), 'Three elements of self-authorship', *Journal of College Student Development*, **49** (4), 269-84.

Beard, Colin and John P. Wilson (2002), *Experiential Learning*, London: Kogan Page.

Bergmann, Jonathan and Aaron Sams (2012), *Flip Your Classroom*, Washington: ISTE.

Biggs, John (2003), *Teaching for Quality Learning at University: What the Student Does*, London: Open University Press.

Bjerke, Bjorn (2007), *Understanding Entrepreneurship*, Cheltenham, UK · Northampton, MA, USA: Edward Elgar.

Blank, Steve abd Bob Dorf (2012), *The Startup Owner's Manual*, California: K & S Ranch.

Boud, David (2001), 'Introduction: Making the Move to Peer Learning', in David Boud R. Cohen and Jane Sampson (eds), *Peer Learning in Higher Education: Learning From & With Each Other*, London: Kogan Page Ltd.

Brandon, Robert N. (1990), *Adaptation and Environment*, New Jersey: Princeton University Press.

Brandon, Robert N. (1996), *Concepts and Methods in Evolutionary Biology*, New York: Cambridge University Press.

Bridge, Simon and C. Hegarty (2012), 'An alternative to business plan-based advice for start-ups?', *Industry and Higher Education*, **26** (6), 443-452.

Bridge, Steven and Cecilia Hegarty (2011), 'An alternative to business plan-based advice for start-ups?', *Proceedings of the 34th Institute of Small Business and Entrepreneurship Conference*, Sheffield, November 9-10.

Brookfield, Stephen (1986), *Understanding and Facilitating Adult Learning*, San Francisco: Jossey-Bass.

Brookfield, Stephen (1990), *The Skillful Teacher*, San Francisco: Jossey-Bass.

Brookes, Simon and Alex Moseley (2012), 'Authentic contextual games for learning', in Nicola Whitton and Alex Moseley (eds), *Using Games to Enhance learning and Teaching: A Beginner's Guide*, London: Routledge.

Bruyat, Chirstin and Pierre-Andre Julien (2001), 'Defining the field of research in entrepreneurship', *Journal of Business Venturing*, **16**, 165-80.

Bygrave, William (2010), *Personal Communications*, 6th August 2010.

Carroll, Lewis (1869), *Alice in Wonderland*, London: MacMillan and Co.

Castaneda, Carlos (1968), *The Teachings of Don Juan – a Yaqui Way of Knowledge,* New York: Ballantine Books.

Christensen, Clayton, Curtis W. Johnson and Michael B. Horn (2008), *Disrupting Class*, New York: McGraw-Hill.

Cranton, Patricia (1994), *Understanding and Promoting Transformative Learning*, San Francisco: Jossey-Bass.

Dewey, John (1933), *How We Think,* Boston: D.C. Heath & Co.

Doren, Mark Van, 'BrainyQuote', http://www.brainyquote.com/quotes/quotes/m/markvandor108042.html, (accessed 10 October 2013).

Drago-Severson, Eleanor (2009), *Leading Adult Learning*, London: Sage.

Dweck, Carol S. (2006), *How We Can Learn to Fulfill Our Potential*, New York: Ballantine Books.

Emerson, Ralph W. (1904), *The Works of Ralph Waldo Emerson*, London: George Bell.

Fayolle, Alain (2007a), *Handbook of Research in Entrepreneurship Education, Volume 1*, Cheltenham, UK · Northampton, MA, USA: Edward Elgar.

Fayolle, Alain (2007b), *Handbook of Research in Entrepreneurship Education, Volume 2*, Cheltenham, UK · Northampton, MA, USA: Edward Elgar.

Fayolle, Alain (2010), *Handbook of Research in Entrepreneurship Education, Volume 3*, Cheltenham, UK · Northampton, MA, USA: Edward Elgar.

Freire, Paulo (1974), *Pedagogy of the Oppressed*, New York: Seabury Press.

Gardner, Howard (1993), *Multiple Intelligences: The Theory in Practice*, New York: Basic Books.

Gibb, Allan (2002), 'Creating conducive environments for learning and entrepreneurship: Living with, dealing with, creating and enjoying uncertainty and complexity', *Industry & Higher Education*, **16** (3), 135–48.

Gladwell, Malcolm (2002), *The Tipping Point*, New York: Little, Brown and Company.

Guillebeau, Chris (2012), *The $100 Startup*, London: MacMillan.

Hannan, Michael T. and John Freeman (1977), 'The population ecology of organizations', *American Journal of Sociology*, **82** (5), 929-64.

Hart, Tobin (2001), *From Information to Transformation*, New York: Peter Lang.

Haskell, Edward F. (1949), 'A clarification of social science', *Main Currents in Modern Thought*, **7**, 45–51.

Heath, Roy (1964), *The Reasonable Adventurer*, Pittsburgh: University of Pittsburgh Press.

Hisrich, Robert D., Michael P. Peters and Dean A. Shepherd (2010), *Entrepreneurship* (8th ed.), New York: McGraw-Hill Irwin.

Honig, Benson (2004), 'Entrepreneurship education: Towards a model of contingency based business planning', *Academy of Management Learning and Education*, **3** (3), 258-273.

Hornak, Anne M. and A. M. Ortiz (2004), 'Promoting self-authorship through an interdisciplinary writing curriculum', in Marcia Baxter-Magolda and P. M. King (eds), *Learning Partnerships*, Virginia: Stylus Publishing.

Hutchings, Pat, M. T. Huber and A. Ciccone (2011), *Scholarship of Teaching and Learning Reconsidered*, San Francisco: Jossey-Bass.

Jones, Colin (2011), *Teaching Entrepreneurship to Undergraduates*, Cheltenham, UK · Northampton, MA, USA: Edward Elgar.

Jones, Colin and H. Matlay (2011). 'Understanding the heterogeneity of entrepreneurship education: Going beyond Gartner', *Education + Training*, **53** (8/9), 692-703.

Jones, Colin and Penaluna, Andy (2013), 'Moving beyond the business plan', *Education + Training*, In Press.

Jones, Colin (2007), 'Using old concepts to gain new insights: Addressing the issue of consistency', *Management Decision*, **45** (1), 29-42.

Kaufman, Josh (2012), *The Personal MBA*, New York: Portfolio Penguin.

Kegan, Robert (1982), *The Evolving Self: Problem and Process in Human Development*, Cambridge, MA: Harvard University Press.

Kegan, Robert (1994), *In Over Our Heads*, London: Harvard University Press.

Ketner, Kenneth L. (1992), Reasoning and the Logic of Things, London: Harvard University Press.

Klug, Beverly J. and P. T. Whitfield (2003), *Widening the Circle*, New York: Routledge.

Knowles, Malcolm S. (1980), *The Modern Practice of Adult Education: From Pedagogy to Andragogy*, Chicago: Follett Publishing.

Kuratko, Donald (2006), 'A tribute to 50 years of excellence in entrepreneurship and small business', *Journal of Small Business Management*, **44** (3), 483-492.

Lange, Julian, A. Mollov, M. Pearlmutter, S. Singh and W.D. Bygrave (2007), 'Pre-startup formal business plans and post-startup performance: A study of 116 new ventures', *Venture Capital Journal*, **9** (4), 1–20.

Lidicker, William Z. (1979), 'A clarification of interactions in ecological systems', *Bioscience*, *29*, 475-75.

MacArthur, Robert H. and Edward O. Wilson (1967), *The Theory of Island Biogeography*, New Jersey: Princeton University Press.

McKenzie, Roderick D. (1934), 'Demography, human geography, and human ecology', in Luther L. Bernard (ed), *The Fields and Methods of Sociology*, New York: Ray Lang & Richard Smith.

Mac Nally, Ralph C. (1995), *Ecological Versatility and Community Ecology*, Melbourne: Cambridge University Press.

Magnusson, Shirley, J. Krajcik and H. Borko (1999), 'Nature, sources and development of pedagogical content knowledge for science teaching', in in Julie Gess-Newsome and Norman G. Lederman (eds), *Examining Pedagogical Content Knowledge*, London: Kluwer Academic Publishers.

Merton, Thomas (1979), *Love and Living*, New York: Farrar, Straus & Giroux.

Merzenich, Michael (2009), 'Growing evidence of brain plasticity', available at: http://www.ted.com/search?cat=ss_all&q=Merzenich.

Meszaros, Peggy S. (2007), 'The journey of self-authorship: Why is it necessary?', *New Directions for Teaching and Learning*, **109**, 5-14.

Mullins, John W. and Komisar, Randy (2009), *Getting To Plan B*, Boston, MA: Harvard Business Press.

Odling-Smee, John F., Kevin N. Laland and Marcus W. Feldman (2003), *Niche Construction: The Neglected Process in Evolution*, Oxford: Princeton University Press.

Odum, Howard T. (1995), *Environmental Accounting, Emergy and Decision Making*, New York: John Wiley.

Palmer, Parker J. (1997), *The Courage to Teach: Exploring the Inner Landscape of a Teacher's Life*, San Francisco: Jossey-Bass.

Pen, Ido, T. Uller, B. Feldmeyer, A. Harts, G. M. While and E. Wapstra (2010), 'Climate driven population divergence in sex-determining systems', *Nature*, **468**, 436-39.

Penaluna, Kathryn, A. Penaluna and C. Jones (2012), 'The context of enterprise education: Insights into current practice', *Industry & Higher Education*, **26** (3), 163-75.

Penrose, Edith (1959), *The Theory of the Growth of the Firm*, New York: John Wiley and Sons.

Pittaway, Luke, P. Hannon, A. Gibb and J. Thompson (2009), 'Assessment in enterprise education', *International Journal of Entrepreneurial Behaviour and Research*, **15** (1), 71-93.

Pittaway, Luke and C. Edwards (2012), 'Assessment: Examining practice in entrepreneurship education', *Education + Training*, **54** (8/9), 778-800.

Porter, Michael E. (1980), *Competitive Strategy*, New York: Free Press.

Porter, Michael E. (1985), *Competitive Advantage*, New York: Free Press.

Proust, Marcel, 'BrainyQuote', http://www.brainyquote.com/quotes/quotes/m/marcelprou107111.html, (accessed on 10 October 2013).

QAA (2012), 'Quality Assurance Agency for Higher Education – Enterprise and entrepreneurship: a new approach to learning', available at: http://www.qaa.ac.uk/Newsroom/PressReleases/Pages/Enterprise-and-entrepreneurship-a-new-approach-to-learning.aspx, (accessed 6 April 2012).

Rankin, Nicholas (2008), *Churchills' Wizards: The British Genius for Deception*, London: Faber & Faber.

Read, Stuart, Saras Sarasvathy, Nick Dew, Robert Wiltbank and Anne-Valerie Ohlsson (2011), *Effectual Entrepreneurship*, London: Routledge.

Ries, Eric (2011), *The Lean Startup*, New York: Crown Business.

Rumsfeld, Donald (2002), 'Rumsfeld baffles press with unknown unknowns', ABC News Online, June 7, 2002, www.abc.net.au/news/newsitems/s576186.htm.

Ruskin, John (1917), *The Stones of Venice*, London: J.M. Dent & Co.

Sarasvathy, Saras D. (2008), *Effectuation: Elements of Entrepreneurial Expertise*, Cheltenham, UK · Northampton, MA, USA: Edward Elgar.

Shane, Shane A. (2008), *The Illusions of Entrepreneurship*, London: Yale University Press.

Shulman, Lee (1986), 'Those who understand: Knowledge growth in teaching', *Educational Researcher,* **15** (2), 4-14.

Skinner, Burrhus F. (1964), 'New methods and new aims in teaching', *New Scientist*, **122**, 483-84.

Stabell, Charles B. and Øystein D. Fjeldstad (1998), 'Configuring value for competitive advantage: on chains, shops, and networks', *Strategic Management Journal*, **19** (5), 413-37.

Stevenson, Howard H., Irving H. Grousbeck, Michael J. Roberts and Amar Bhide (1999), *New Business Ventures and the Entrepreneur*, (5th ed.), McGraw-Hill.

Sumner, William G. (1902), *Earth Hunger and Other Essays*, New Haven: Yale University Press.

Taylor, Kathleen (2000), 'Teaching with developmental intention', in Jack Mezirow (ed.), *Learning as Transformation: Critical Perspectives on a Theory in Progress*, San Francisco: Jossey-Bass.

Thomas, Michael S. C. (2012), 'Brain plasticity and education', *Educational Neuroscience*, **1** (1), 143-56.

Tyler, Ralph (1949), *Basic Principles of Curriculum and Instruction*, Chicago: The University of Chicago Press.

Van Valen, Leigh (1973), 'A New Evolutionary Law', *Evolutionary Theory*, **1**, 1-30.

Veblen, Thorstein (1919), *The Place of Science in Modern Civilization*, New York: B. W. Huebsch.

Veblen, Thorstein (1922), *The Theory of the Leisure Class*, New York: MacMillan Company.

Walter, Gimme H. (2013), 'Autecology and the balance of nature – ecological laws and human-induced invasions', in Klaus Rohde (ed.), *The Balance of Nature and Human Impact, Melbourne*: Cambridge University Press.

Wankel, Charles (2010), *Cutting-Edge Social Media Approaches to Business Education*, Charlotte, NC: IAP.

Whitehead, Alfred N. (1929), *The Aims of Education and Other Essays*, New York: The Free Press.

Wlodkowski, Raymond J. (1999), *Enhancing Adult Motivation to Learn*, San Francisco: Jossey-Bass.

# Index